The Orange Order

MERVYN JESS is a senior broadcast journalist with BBC Northern Ireland who has reported and written extensively on Orange issues in a career spanning thirty years. He was born in County Down where he continues to live.

THE ORANGE ORDER

MERVYN JESS

THE O'BRIEN PRESS

DUBLIN

First published 2007 by The O'Brien Press Ltd,
12 Terenure Road East, Rathgar, Dublin 6, Ireland.
Tel: +353 1 4923333; Fax: +353 1 4922777
E-mail: books@obrien.ie
Website: www.obrien.ie

ISBN: 978-0-86278-996-1

British Library Cataloguing in Publication Data
Jess, Mervyn
The Orange Order
1. Orange Order - History
2. Religion and politics - Northern Ireland
3. Unionism (Irish politics) - History
4. Orangemen - Ireland - History
5. Northern Ireland - Politics and government
6. Ireland - History
I. Title
941.6

1 2 3 4 5 6 7 8
07 08 09 10 11

Editing, typesetting, layout and design: The O'Brien Press Ltd
Printed and bound in the UK by J.H. Haynes & Co Ltd, Sparkford

Picture Credits: cover © Corbis; p. 1 (top) © Mervyn Jess; p.1 (bottom) and p. 2
(bottom) © Press Eye; p. 2 (top) © Austin Hunter; p. 3 (top), p. 4 (both), p. 5
(bottom) © Photocall Ireland; p. 3 (bottom), p. 5 (top), pp 6-8 (all) © Pacemaker
Press International.

To my parents

ACKNOWLEDGEMENTS

When this project was first proposed at the beginning of 2006 it was intended to be a much smaller publication, but the intervening months have seen it grow into the book you hold in your hands now. Telling the story of the Orange Order is a challenge in a number of respects. Members of the organisation have traditionally been wary of the media and getting them to talk openly about a fraternity that they hold dear to their hearts and that they perceive to be under constant attack and unfair scrutiny is no easy matter.

Metaphorically speaking, when a writer first walks through the door of a lodge-room, there are a surprising number of other doors leading off into all sorts of different rooms. The difficulty with a shorter book is not having the time and space to explore these other rooms, each of which is an important component in the history of an organisation that has been at the heart of Anglo-Irish affairs from its formation to the present day.

This publication does not pretend to be a definitive history, but it does provide a window into what has traditionally been an overly protective and secretive organisation. Some of those at the highest level within the Order agreed to be interviewed for the book; their views are contrasted with their most outspoken opponents and the mix is complemented by a historical perspective from more independent observers. This is a book for the uninitiated in Orangeism, and also for those in the pro- and anti- camps, but most importantly it should be read by anyone seeking to understand the historical significance of the Orange Order and where it is going in the twenty-first century.

My thanks go to all those – too many in number to acknowledge individually – who have helped me gain an invaluable insight into the workings of a complex institution. Some are identified and named in the text. Others are not. All, from Orange, Black and Green backgrounds, have my appreciation for their time, patience and expertise. Any errors of fact or interpretation are mine alone.

There are numerous other people who assisted me who did not wish to be identified, and to them I also bear a debt of gratitude.

Thanks go to Andrew Colman, Head of News and Current Affairs – BBC Northern Ireland, for allowing me the latitude to complete this work. Also to my journalist colleagues Seamus Kelters and Brian Rowan for their support and advice throughout the project.

My gratitude is also extended to the team at The O'Brien Press for helping to conceive the idea and their encouragement at every stage of the process. In particular I would like to thank Helen Carr and Emer Ryan for scrutinising my numerous drafts and giving expert advice and direction.

I also want to acknowledge the love and support of my family – my wife Lynn and daughters Aimee and Melanie, who coaxed and cajoled me to complete the project as the publisher's deadline drew ever nearer. Also my mother, Rosemary, who impressed upon me from an early age the importance of reading and writing and my late father Hans Gilmore Jess – an Orangeman and a Blackman – who encouraged his children to think for themselves and not to take anything at face value.

That advice has been invaluable during my journalistic career in Northern Ireland over the past thirty years and was a factor in my decision to write this book, a task which has proven both challenging and stimulating. Initially, I was apprehensive about taking on a subject that, frankly, could have filled a hundred books. I have attempted to reflect not only views from within, but also from outside the institution and in doing so I believe I've managed to shine a light into its darker recesses, which are rarely visited. Ultimately, the reader will make their own judgement regarding that and indeed the subject matter of this book – the Orange Order itself.

CONTENTS

PROLOGUE

Joining the Orange Order is a big step in the life of young Protestant men. It involves a major decision by anyone intending to become a member of an institution that is among the oldest surviving fraternities in the world. The membership procedure is similar wherever Orangeism is active. When a man applies or is invited to join a lodge, he is asked along to one of the hundreds of Orange halls scattered across the country. It could be a small, dimly lit corrugated-iron hut in a rural setting, well away from the main roads and up a hedge-lined lane, or it might be in a major conurbation on the corner of a busy city street. In larger lodges, dozens of brethren – with ages ranging from eighteen to eighty – might be present. In the smallest, a much-needed new candidate could find himself standing in a lodge room with fewer than a dozen members present. The initiation ceremony is the same regardless. The candidate is brought before the Worshipful Master, officers and lodge brethren. He then becomes the focus of attention in an initiation ritual, handed down and performed over two centuries. Part of that ritual includes the reading of the Qualifications of an Orangeman. They are as follows:

An Orangeman should have a sincere love and veneration for his Heavenly Father; a humble and steadfast faith in Jesus Christ, the Saviour of mankind, believing in Him as the only Mediator between God and man. He should cultivate truth and justice, brotherly kindness and charity, devotion and piety, concord and unity, and obedience to the laws; his deportment should be gentle and compassionate, kind and courteous; he should seek the society of the virtuous, and avoid that of the evil; he should honour and diligently study the Holy Scriptures, and make them the rule of his faith and practice; he should love, uphold, and defend the Protestant religion, and sincerely desire and endeavour to propagate its doctrines and precepts; he should strenuously oppose the fatal errors and doctrines of the Church of Rome, and scrupulously avoid countenancing (by his presence or otherwise) any act or ceremony of Popish worship; he should, by all lawful means, resist the ascendancy of that Church, its encroachments and the extension of its power, ever abstaining from all uncharitable words, actions, or sentiments towards his Roman Catholic brethren; he should remember to keep holy the Sabbath day, and attend the public worship of God, and diligently train up his offspring, and all under his control, in the fear of God, and in the Protestant faith; he should never take the name of God in vain, but abstain from all cursing and profane language, and use every opportunity of discouraging these, and other sinful practices, in others; his conduct should be guided by wisdom and prudence, and marked by honesty, temperance and sobriety; the glory of God and the welfare of man, the honour of his Sovereign and the good of his country, should be the motive of his actions.

CHAPTER 1

THE BEGINNING

Dan Winter's house is a small whitewashed, mud-walled thatched cottage near the village of Loughgall in County Armagh's orchard country. It is a picture straight out of a tourism brochure: the sort of Irish idyll that attracts hundreds of thousands of people from around the world to visit these shores. This particular cottage, however, has historical foundations that are very different from those of rural Catholic Ireland which invoke images of farming families gathered round open turf fires playing traditional music with a picture of the Virgin Mary and a crucifix hanging on the wall. The walls of the Winter family home are adorned with emblems of another faith, because this dwelling at the Diamond is a historically important bastion of Protestantism – the birthplace of the Orange Order.

Hilda Winter is the widow of Derek Winter – the great, great, great, great-grandson of 'Diamond' Dan Winter – and she is the curator of Dan Winter's House Ancestral Home museum. Upon arrival at this farmer's cottage on Derryloughan Road near Loughgall, the visitors eye is drawn to a flat rock by the half-door in the porch, with the words 'Please come in' painted on it. Inside, the small stone-floored rooms with their low-beamed ceilings and tiny windows are home to a collection of Orange memorabilia dating from the present day back to 1795.

The Winter family has lived here since the eighteenth century but interest in the cottage as a historic site gathered momentum during the 1990 celebrations of the 300th anniversary of the Battle of the Boyne.

'Up until the mid-nineties this was a working turkey farm,' says Hilda Winter, who is seated beside a roaring log fire. 'And this fire was kept going by burning the feathers.'

The museum is run on voluntary donations and gets up to three thousand visitors a year. Visiting Orange lodges have held meetings in the room where the 'founding fathers' discussed the tenets of the Order. In the grassy fields in front of Winter's cottage, on 21 September 1795, a collection of men from non-Catholic denominations linked arms and agreed to band together in defence of what they saw as the Freedom of the Reformed Protestant faith. Among them were Presbyterians, Episcopalians, Quakers, Huguenots and Independents. They had just tasted victory in what became known as the Battle of the Diamond.

Their adversaries were the Roman Catholic Defenders – a vigilante group that had grown out of the violent sectarian confrontations over commerce and land in that part of Mid-Ulster.

These agrarian groups had been at each other's throats since the 1780s. The ruthless Protestant gangs called themselves the Peep o'Day Boys because of their tactic of raiding Catholic homes at the break of dawn to catch their quarry by surprise. The Catholics formed themselves into the Defenders, a group that was also prone to going on the offensive.

Lives and property were destroyed during the period leading up to the confrontation at the Diamond. There had been attempts by both sides at reconciliation. A group calling itself the Council of Seven, including prominent people in the Protestant community and Catholic priests, managed to negotiate a truce, but it was short-lived. The fighting in County Armagh came to a head on two hillsides in the townland of Grange Lower, around a hamlet know as the Diamond. It was Monday, 21 September 1795. The Catholic Defenders lined up on Faughart Hill while the Protestants arranged themselves on the opposite side of the valley, on Diamond Hill. Folklore has it that the Defenders fired the first shot. It is of little consequence. The battle was over in minutes and the Defenders were defeated. The death toll on the Catholic side is estimated at between sixteen and sixty. Orange historians say that the Protestants left the field of battle without one single fatality and only one window in the Winter family home broken. The five victorious leaders gathered in a circle, linked hands and declared their brotherhood in loyalty to the Crown, the country and the reformed Protestant religion. These founding fathers of Orangeism included James Wilson from Dyan in Tyrone, James Sloan from nearby Loughgall and 'Diamond' Dan Winter who, along with his sons, had fought to defend their property in the vicinity of the confrontation.

It was to the Winter's farm cottage that the 'fathers' went to discuss their next move. It was agreed to form a society that would later become the Loyal Orange Institution of Ireland. In the circumstances it was felt, however, that further discussions should take place at a location further removed from the field of battle, in case of reprisals.

Former schoolmaster James Sloan, viewed by his contemporaries as an educated man, was appointed secretary. He owned an inn in nearby Loughgall and it was to this hostelry that the leaders retired later on the day of the battle for further meetings on the formation of the Orange Institution.

In the days immediately following the fighting, the first formal meeting of Orangemen took place in Sloan's Inn at Loughgall. Among those present was Captain John Gifford of the Royal Dublin Militia who was barracked in Portadown. The army had kept a low profile before and during the Battle of the Diamond. It is thought that Captain Gifford was supportive of the Protestant cause and was confident that they would be victorious – so he turned a blind eye to the impending violence and left them to get on with it. The fact that he was at the Sloan Inn meeting and played an important role in the proceedings supports that theory.

The English Catholic historian Plowden credits Gifford with bestowing the title of 'Orangemen' on the brotherhood. He also attributes to him the original obligation and regulations of this new society of Protestant men. Evidence of the Captain's apparent dislike of Catholicism can be found in a letter Gifford wrote to a military colleague stationed in Dublin. The letter, written a few days after the Sloan Inn meeting, refers to the founding in Loughgall of 'a society that for generations would curb both Pope and Popery in Ireland'. It would appear that it was Gifford who first drew the comparison between what the Diamond men had done and what the soldiers of William of Orange had fought for at the Battle of the Boyne nearly a century earlier. It is believed that this comparison went some way towards deciding on the title of Orangemen to refer to the members of the newly formed society.

The Orange title had been in use long before this period. Boyne Societies in commemoration of King William of Orange and his victory over Catholic King James were already in existence. A Protestant Orange Boys' Club was started in County Tyrone in 1792 by James Wilson – a relative of Diamond Dan Winter.

Jonathan Mattison is the Convenor of the Orange Order's Education Committee. He is also an Orange historian who completed his doctorate at Queen's University Belfast, on nineteenth-century Irish Orangeism. 'The foundation of the Order was officially in 1795; however there had been a number of rural and popular Protestant organisations and spells of Orangeism from the 1690s onwards, including Orange Societies and Clubs,' he says. 'During the Tyrconnell period in 1687-88 when he tried to change the make-up of city councils across Ireland, a lot of Protestants and Anglicans were thrown out of the Corporations and Councils. One of the most famous incidents was in Dublin where many Protestants were forced off the City Corporation. They formed their own Society or club known as the Aldermen of Skinners Alley. This is regarded as the starting point in Ireland of a Protestant/Orange-orientated society.'

The early part of the eighteenth century saw the formation of a number of Boyne Societies and Boyne Clubs in Counties Down and Wicklow as well as in Dublin city. The latter part of the century saw the formation of The Peep o'Day Boys who were the most violent Protestant grouping at that time. The vigilante style association was formed in County Armagh following the relaxation of the Penal Laws which had discriminated against Roman Catholics. The grouping was almost exclusively Anglican (Church of Ireland) and it existed to counter economic competition from Catholics over land leases, rents and the production of linen. The 'Boys' were also referred to as 'Protestant Boys', 'Orangemen' and 'Wreckers' due to their modus operandi of smashing the weaving looms in Catholic homes. Throughout the 1790s, the Peep o'Day Boys were held responsible for the expulsion of thousands of Catholics from their homes in central Ulster. It is also claimed that these Anglican extremists did not confine their attacks to Catholics, with Protestant dissenters such as Presbyterians and Quakers being targeted. Critics of Orangeism would argue that the Peep o'Day Boys were the forerunners of the Orange Order, however, there is another view that while some 'Boys' undoubtedly joined Orange lodges, they found themselves in a markedly different association.

According to Mattison, 'The Orange Order, in literal terms, set itself up as a defensive organisation to defend Irish Protestantism and hearth and home.'

Another who attended those early meetings of Orangemen at Sloan's Inn was James Wilson of Dyan. He managed to secure permission for the very first Orange lodge warrant issued. To this day, Loyal Orange Lodge No. 1 Dyan, near

Caledon in County Tyrone, remains a bone of contention amongst the men from the Diamond area of Loughgall in County Armagh. Like their predecessors, they feel that the first warrant should have gone to a local lodge as their men were more directly involved in the Battle of the Diamond. It is reported that they were so upset at not getting the No.1 warrant at the time of the Battle that they sulked and refused to take up any warrant. By the time they had thawed, they were issued with a warrant for Loyal Orange Lodge No. 118. If ever there was an early example of the Ulster 'prods' suffering for their own renowned stubbornness, then this is it.

As a degree of compensation for this indignity, James Sloan, the Loughgall innkeeper who had facilitated these early tentative meetings of Orangemen, is regarded as being the Order's first leader, maybe for no other reason than that he held the keys to the 'Orange Hall'. Initially Sloan, as leader, issued handwritten warrants to newly formed lodges but this would soon be formalised with the creation of a Grand Lodge and the printing of lodge warrants.

The rural and bloody simplicity of the beginnings of an organisation that was to go on to span the world is part of what attracts those with an interest in history to the Winters' cottage today.

'We get all sorts coming here,' says the curator. 'When my husband was alive and this was still our home and a working farm, it was mostly visiting Orangemen. But now we have people from as far away as America, bus loads of tourists on the Irish history trail and students whose studies include the Orange Order.'

Somewhat surprisingly Hilda Winter is not an Orange-woman herself. She is, however, heavily involved with the work of the Women's Institute in her local parish church where, she says, she 'is strengthened by her faith in the Lord.' She takes great pride in her Ulster Protestantism and her family's place in its historical background, and has dedicated herself to preserving that part of the history of Orangeism that literally landed on her doorstep. She is well read on the subject and has carried out much of the research into her own family history and the Battle of the Diamond.

When explaining to visitors what happened at the Diamond over two hundred years ago, Hilda Winter's style is less a lecture in history and more of 'a story round the fireplace'.

'When the men met in the days after the "Battle of the Diamond" to form their Orange society they didn't want the Peep o'Day Boys in it, even though they fought in the Battle,' she explains. 'They were too vicious, too violent.'

While these vigilantes weren't officially incorporated into the new Orange Institution, it is reasonable to assume that some the Peep o'Day Boys managed to slip through the net.

The forming of a fraternal bond was less problematic amongst the other co-combatants such as the Protestant Orange Boys' Club from Dyan in Tyrone. According to Hilda Winter,

'Those from the Dyan Club who fought at the Diamond always said they went into Battle as Orange Boys and came out as Orangemen.'

CHAPTER 2

THE FIRST 200 YEARS

Shallow understanding from people of good will is more frustrating than
absolute misunderstanding from people of ill-will.
— *Martin Luther King Jnr*

In spite of its constitution and stated objectives, and the attempts of many of its members to live up to what the Order expects of them, as an institution it has never been far from conflict. At times, that conflict has been with Catholics contesting their competing religious and civil rights, which they saw being trampled on by Orange feet. More intriguing perhaps and certainly less well-publicised have been the periodic but continual conflicts within a Loyal Order composed of sharply differing individuals and splintered interest groups.

Institute of Conflict Research Director, Neil Jarman, says,

> I think one of the fascinating things about the Orange Order is that it has managed to stay together as a single organisation. You could say it is misunderstood, but that's assuming it has a single rationale or raison d'être. I don't

think it does and I'm not sure that it ever did. Its success is based on the fact that it can mean different things to different people at the same time. If you look at any other organisation what tends to happen is that it starts off as a democratically controlled grassroots movement, and over the years becomes institutionalised. The power moves vertically and you end up in a very centralised and controlled organisation. What's interesting with the Orange is that it has remained largely de-centralised for over two hundred years and on that level it is interesting the way those competing tendencies have been maintained. Clearly there's a central committee (Grand Lodge), but it doesn't have the authority to issue dictates and even when it does (i.e. no contact with the Parades Commission) people tend to ignore the dictate and do it anyway. That's one of the interesting things that hasn't really been explored about the Order – how it actually managed to sustain that democratic appeal and while not becoming ossified.

The mixed and at times conflicting messages that emerge from Orangeism are probably symptomatic of the diverse nature of the many lodges that make up the Order. It is generally acknowledged that rural lodges tend to have a different way of looking at things from urban lodges. That distinction can also be extended to those members who have risen through the ranks and view Orangeism from the lofty heights of Grand Lodge.

'They're certainly linked but they're different,' says Jarman.

'The fact that the Order has had all those different perspectives and sets of relationships means that it is almost certainly misunderstood by nearly everybody.'

GROWING PAINS

What was to become known as the Loyal Orange Institution of Ireland grew at a pace. District and County lodges were formed and the membership was, in those early days, drawn mostly from the labouring and artisan classes. Viscount Northland from Dungannon was one of the few landed gentry to join. The professional classes attending lodge meetings included ex-army officers and Protestant clergy – among them the Rev. George Maunsell, the Rector of Drumcree parish church near Portadown. More than two centuries later, a series of events around that particular parish church would have a major influence in shaping the future of the Orange Order.

The rapid growth of Orangeism also led to a proliferation of different rules and regulations for various lodges across the country. It soon dawned on people that there was a need for uniformity. On 12 July 1796, a meeting was held in Portadown where the idea of a Grand Lodge was put forward for consideration. On that same day, the first Orange Order parades took place in Portadown, Lurgan and Waringstown.

In 1797, in Dublin, Thomas Verner, who was already the Grand Master of Tyrone, Londonderry and Fermanagh, founded Lodge No. 176 and in less than a year it had more than three hundred members. The roll call read like a page from Burke's Peerage and these names were to form the nucleus of the new Grand Lodge of Ireland. Verner himself was to become the first

Orangeman to occupy the Grand Master's chair. On 8 March the following year, a meeting was called to discuss it. Nine lodges represented by eighteen Orangemen attended. As an indication of the Order's historically close ties with the Crown forces, fourteen of the delegates at the meeting were serving members of County Militia across Ireland. As a consequence, those involved in drawing up the twelve resolutions for the formation of the Grand Orange Lodge of Ireland included one lieutenant colonel, one major, two captains, two warrant officers, eight sergeants and four civilians.

FORMATION OF THE GRAND LODGE

On 9 April 1798, the Grand Orange Lodge of Ireland was finally formed at Thomas Verner's Georgian townhouse in Dawson Street in Dublin. As the nobility mixed with army officers, sipping vintage wines and congratulating each other in the stately drawing rooms after the Grand Lodge meeting, a County Armagh farmer looking on could have been forgiven for thinking that it was all far removed from the 'muck and gutters and porter' at Dan Winter's cottage or Sloan's tavern.

By 1798, even larger Orange parades were being held in Belfast, Lisburn and Lurgan. In Lurgan, the most senior military officer in Ulster, Lieutenant General Lake, the General Officer Commanding, inspected the parade. In many respects this would have been seen as a very public seal of approval by the authorities for the Orange Institution. It was significant that the Orangemen were fully behind the Crown and helped defeat the rebellion by the United Irishmen that year. There were consequences to flow from the 1798 Rebellion that would leave many of the rank and file of the Order in dismay. After the Rebellion had been put down, the British Prime Minister, William Pitt the Younger, decided that it would be best to unify the London and Dublin governments. The loyal Orangemen saw the removal of the mainly Protestant Irish parliament as a major blow to the Protestant ascendancy.

The Orange Grand Master, Thomas Verner, was in favour of Pitt's plan to unify the parliaments, but he was conscious that many of his brethren were not. It was felt that adopting a neutral stance on this controversial issue would be best to maintain good relations within the Order. Consequently the Grand Lodge of Ireland issued statements in December 1798, and again the following month, advising Orangemen 'strictly to abstain from expressing any opinion, pro or con, upon the question of a legislative union between Ireland and Great Britain', because such expressions of opinion and such discussion in lodges would lead only to 'disunion'.

Emotions were running high on the question of legislative union and some Orange lodges in Dublin declared, 'We consider the extinction of our separate legislatures as the extinction of the Irish nation.' There was also growing resentment in the north·of Ireland. Lodge meetings denounced the proposed changes of the Irish Parliament and the Grand Lodge's attitude to it. All the resolutions put forward by the Ulster lodges were against the Union of the parliaments of Ireland and Great Britain. Orangemen who were members of the Dublin parliament threw their weight firmly behind the anti-union movement. Within three years, what had begun as small 'band of brothers' skirmishing in the fields and muddy ditches of County Armagh had evolved into a major political force in Ireland.

CATHOLIC OPPOSITION

By August 1800, the Act of Union had been passed in Parliament and the following January it became law. Paradoxically, while many Orangemen had been suspicious and hostile to the plans to unify the Dublin and London parliaments, when it came into being they were to pledge undying loyalty to it. Many in the Protestant community, however, still had concerns about the demands for Roman Catholic emancipation. Across the water in Great Britain, a growing number of English politicians had begun to view the treatment of Catholics in Ireland by their Protestant neighbours as unfair, to say the least. This appears to have galvanised Orange political thinking at the time. The then Grand Master, the Right Hon. George Ogle (1801–1818) and his fellow Orange members of Parliament found themselves constantly defending their corner at Westminster against MPs who were sympathetic to the cause of Catholic emancipation.

In 1823, Daniel O'Connell founded the Catholic Association, which waged a campaign that would impinge on Anglo–Irish politics for the next twenty years. All Irish citizens were encouraged to join the Association by paying a 'Catholic rent' of a penny a month to help finance its activities. The money was collected at Sunday Mass in churches, and large numbers of Catholics throughout Ireland joined the Association.

At home, as at Westminster, the Orange Order found itself on the defensive in the face of political revisionism. Lodges were moving away from their earlier incarnations as 'fighting societies' and were evolving into political and fraternity clubs. But the sensitive political climate created by O'Connell's Catholic Association activities kept the Order's leadership on its toes in efforts to avoid a propaganda disaster. Orange displays and parades were kept to a minimum so as not to upset the fragile peace that existed in some parts of Ireland. The Grand Secretary of the Grand Lodge of Ireland, Patrick Duigenan, and the Grand Treasurer, Sir Richard Musgrave, are credited with maintaining cohesiveness within the Order at this time and making sure that the membership was focused and moving forward.

In March 1823, the County Armagh Grand Lodge issued the following statement:

> We feel not less surprised than grieved that Orange associations should be accused of illegal interference in the state, or branded as an intolerant and persecuting faction. Where in this land have the laws been so well enforced and so cheerfully obeyed as in those districts where the Orange association has more power and influence?

The Orangemen had a powerful ally in the English parliamentarian Robert Peel. Peel recognised the value of organised groups of loyalists in Ireland who would willingly swell the ranks of local yeomanry if needed to discourage rebellion or internecine conflict in the country. When, as Sir Robert Peel, he became Chief Secretary for Ireland, the Orangemen knew that they had at least one 'friend in high places'. During his two years in office as Chief Secretary, the Order came under numerous attacks and he did what he could to help. Those supporting O'Connell's campaign were quick to seize on what they saw as this partiality towards Protestants and bestowed on Sir Robert the sobriquet 'Orange Peel'.

Since 1815, the institution had been racked by internal disputes over issues such as lodge ritual. External developments were to forge the bickering parties into a more unified force in the face of adversity. The agrarian troubles of the 1820s, the new Vice-Regal power in Dublin and its views on Orangeism, and the resurgence of Daniel O'Connell's campaign were the embodiment of that adversity.

By 1820, Grand Lodge was meeting twice a year in February and August and a committee had been appointed to oversee matters in between times. A new set of rules and regulations was drafted and published to stymie any further fracturing of the Orange fraternity over attempts to form 'higher orders'. The rules stated that an Orangeman 'could not assist at nor sanction the making of any member in any other Order purporting to be part of the Orange system, than the Orange and Purple'.

UNLAWFUL OATH ACT

In July 1823, Parliament passed the Unlawful Oath Act. It was primarily aimed at the Catholic Ribbonmen, a secretive, oath-bound organisation, which used violence, including arson and the maiming of livestock, to resist higher rents and evictions. The Ribbonmen were mostly farm labourers armed with cudgels and bludgeons and they were recognisable by a green ribbon worn in their buttonholes. The anti-Protestant, anti-British association was formed in the early part of the nineteenth century and combined members of existing Catholic agrarian groups. These included the Defenders who had been active in pursuit of Catholic interests in the northern counties of Ireland and the Whiteboys – so-called because they wore roughly woven white linen tops – who had waged a guerrilla war in the south against what they saw as the injustices of landlordism.

The government's net, however, was cast wide and it caught Orangemen as well as Ribbonmen. A new Constitution and Rules book was published to meet the legal requirements of the Act, and Grand Lodge even went so far as to prohibit Twelfth demonstrations. This was a risky strategy. The Orange hierarchy was in danger of alienating the grassroots membership. By denying private lodges the opportunity to parade on 12 July, they could have driven the more militant members into the ranks of extremist and less law-abiding Protestant secret societies.

The Order's leaders were basically asking their brethren not to do anything that would bring the Orange into conflict with the powers of the land. It would appear that most of the Orangemen did as they were asked, although in a membership estimated at more than eighty thousand it was inevitable there would be exceptions.

In 1824, O'Connell's Catholic Association had garnered so much support in Ireland that the government feared that it was about to take over the country, despite the group's stated aim of political rather than physical force. The following year, the Unlawful Societies Act was passed, outlawing certain named 'political organisations'. The Catholic Association was among them, as was the Orange Order.

DISSOLVED

On 18 March 1825 – thirty years after its formation – the Orange Institution dissolved itself. A statement released by Grand Lodge to all Orange lodges read:

> At no period was the Institution in a more flourishing condition, or more highly respectable in the number added to its ranks. Notwithstanding which, the Parliament of the United Kingdom have considered it necessary that all political societies should be dissolved. Of course, our society is included. It therefore becomes our duty to inform you that any lodge meeting after this date commits a breach of the law.

Many Orangemen read the Grand Lodge statement, considered it and continued meeting.

'The nineteenth century wasn't all plain sailing for the institution,' says Jonathan Mattison. 'The Unlawful Oaths Act largely targeted nationalist groups in Ireland but it caught the Orange as well and the institution was forced into abeyance in 1825 and it did not return officially until 1828.'

Some lodges burned their warrants and flags in protest but in many rural areas Orange lodges carried on regardless. According to Mattison, there is also evidence that Orange associations tried to exploit loopholes in the Act by reforming themselves as shooting or rifle clubs, which were still legal.

'It was just another way round the law,' he says. 'In my own lodge we have a large silver medal dated 1836 which has the name sporting or rifle club stamped on it. It's the only medal of its kind that I've come across that is physical proof of what was happening at that time.'

The Order's nemesis, the Catholic Association, also found ways of flouting the law and it grew stronger, with Daniel O'Connell being elected to Westminster as MP for County Clare in 1828. He was now in a position to bring his considerable influence to bear on the Prime Minister, the Duke of Wellington, to press for an Act of Catholic Emancipation. The Act became law in 1829.

By now, the Unlawful Societies Act had lapsed and Orange lodges were meeting lawfully once again but with a renewed sense of purpose after Catholic Emancipation. In times of great political uncertainty the different sectors of the electorate have historically rallied round their respective flags. Protestants, who feared being overrun by Catholics in Ireland, turned to the Orange Institution for guidance and protection. The institution found itself engaged in battles on several fronts at once.

In Ireland, Orangemen were once more calling for the restoration of their 'right to parade.' The leadership however had got too far in front of its troops and as the battle began, it was in danger of being cut off. Senior figures in the Orange appeared concerned only with weighty issues such as the Constitution, repeal of the laws and the issue of the established church in Ireland. The rank-and-file membership was concerned only with having the right to parade restored.

At Westminster, the Whig government was dependent on the support of Daniel O'Connell and the radicals to stay in power. In 1836, the government decided to move against the Orange Institution and, in February, King William IV declared that he would be 'pleased to take such measures as may be seen to be advisable for the effectual discouragement of Orange lodges and generally of all political societies that exclude persons of different religious faith, that use secret signs and symbols and act by means of associated branches.' The Grand Lodge gave the government an assurance that immediate steps would be taken to dissolve the Loyal Orange Institution.

As they had done eleven years earlier, many lodges throughout Ireland, particularly in the north of the country, refused to countenance dissolution and it was business as usual. Once more Armagh came to the fore. In a resolution dated 13 June 1836, the Armagh County Grand Lodge voted that 'the business of the Institution in this country be entrusted, as in the early days, to Grand Lodge of the same (Armagh), until Grand Lodge of Ireland resumes its function.'

In November the following year, the Grand Lodge of Ireland was reconstructed in Dublin with Lord Roden – a member of the landed gentry with an estate outside Newcastle, County Down – appointed Grand Master. In 1844, when the Union of Ireland and Great Britain was once again in question, a Grand Lodge of Ulster was formed to give 'mutual support and defence in these perilous times'. When the Grand Lodge met in Enniskillen in August of the following year, the Earl of Enniskillen took over the reigns as Grand Master.

Orange historian and the Order's Education Committee Convenor, Jonathan Mattison, explains how, when the Law changed in 1844, the 'gentry leadership' returned to the Order which had been sustained by the grassroots membership who had continued with the task in hand despite the pressures on them:

> You could argue that the gentry wanted to get back in so they could control the future development of the Order rather than being apart from it and having no influence whatsoever. That ten-year period in the 1830s, when more middle-class and more bourgeois elements take up leadership roles, benefits the Order. There was a limited aristocracy in Ireland compared to England, so it was more landed gentry around the Armagh area who got involved at first. Then as the Institution spread, a large number of the minor gentry came on board. During the late 1870s and early 1880s, around the time of the Land War in Ireland, a lot of the larger gentry became members of the institution.

According to Mattison, the threat of Home Rule, the land war and the disestablishment of the Church of Ireland meant that 'every Protestant felt like they were under the cosh'. What would be described now as 'Ulster Protestant paranoia' was widespread. 'They'd suffered a series of knocks and they felt that their backs were against the wall.' The Orange Order continued to grow as a national organisation. 'At that time there was an Orange presence in twenty-six counties across Ireland.'

CLASH AT DOLLY'S BRAE
In the spring of 1849 the Ribbonmen, who were sworn enemies of the Orange Order, were particularly active in County Down. A man was killed man   near Katesbridge   and

Orangemen were attacked in Crossgar. The mutual animosity between the two organisations would eventually lead to a much larger confrontation and more bloodshed. The Ribbonmen and the Orangemen clashed during an Orange parade at Dolly's Brae near Castlewellan. The incident had certain characteristics which where to surface much later during parades in the 1980s and 1990s.

In *Orangeism, a new historical appreciation,* Dewar, Brown and Long state that the parade had become a point of honour with the local Orangemen to show their determination and strength by marching over the Brae by the old road, where masses of armed Ribbonmen had crowded to prevent them. Escorted by troops and police, and with two priests helping to restrain the Ribbonmen, they did so. On the return journey a squib went off and two shots were fired. Military and police witnesses swore that these came from the hill where the Ribbonmen had stayed all day. A volley was fired at soldiers, police and Orangemen. They cleared the hill under fire and two lodges planted their flags on the top. Lives were lost, houses were burned and Orangemen were said to have acted savagely.

Estimates put the number of people killed that day at between thirty and eighty and most of the dead were said to be Ribbonmen. The clash on the Brae prompted more legislation and, in 1850, the Party Processions Act was passed, making it illegal to hold meetings, which would 'tend to provoke animosity between different classes of Her Majesty's subjects'. In effect it put a stop to Protestant and Catholic organisations marching on their special days.

According to historian Dr Eamon Phoenix, the fallout from the Dolly's Brae confrontation cannot be underestimated:

> The introduction of the Party Processions Act was a big moment. It applied to all sorts of political processions, both Orange and Green. By the 1860s, Orangemen in the north of Ireland were complaining that it was being rigidly imposed in Ulster against Orange parades but disregarded in other parts of Ireland where Repealer parades and pro-Fenian-type gatherings were taking place.

JOHNSTON OF BALLYKILBEG

It was seventeen years before that law was tested by Protestants, and the distinctive bearded features of the man responsible are still commemorated on Orange lodge banners. William Johnston, a lawyer and staunch Orangeman from Ballykilbeg in south Down, led a parade of Orangemen from the market town of Newtownards to the seaside resort of Bangor in County Down on 12 July 1867.

Johnston is believed to have chosen this parade route for a number of reasons. Firstly, he had the support of the County Grand Lodge of Down. Secondly, it would take place close to the working-class Orange power-base of Belfast from which it would draw support and thirdly, it was a staunchly Protestant area and unlikely to cause offence to large numbers of Catholics, which would have strengthened the hand of the authorities in taking action to stop it. The march nevertheless, was in clear breach of the legislation. Up to a hundred lodges and an estimated forty thousand marchers and spectators took part in the protest. Only William Johnston and a handful of others were prosecuted. So intent was Johnston on making his mark that he refused to pay the bail money that would have secured his release. When he emerged from Downpatrick jail a month later, thousands of supporters had gathered at the gates, singing Orange songs as loyalist bands played their party tunes.

Johnston had flown his flag not only in the face of the law but also in the face of Grand Lodge; the support he received from the rank and file proved that he was not a lone voice among Orangeism. Senior figures within the Order were less than impressed, though, with what they saw as this flagrant breach of policy and discipline. However, it seems that Johnston did not give a 'fife and drum', so to speak.

THE MASTER AND THE MAN

As the nineteenth century proceeded towards its conclusion, the politics of Ireland and Great Britain were to determine the direction the Order was travelling. Constant sniping by politicians and the ban on parades had left many Orangemen in the doldrums.

The offhand and sometimes hostile attitude of the Anglo-Irish gentry was not helping the Orange causes either, as Eamon Phoenix explains:

> Pre-1850s, Orangeism was very much a Church of Ireland labourers' organisation with some support from the landed gentry dating back to the 1790s and the challenge of the United Irishmen. Most Anglo-Irish landlords, especially in the north, would have looked upon Orangeism

with disdain. Hugh Montgomery, of Blessingburn House in Fivemiletown, wrote a famous letter around 1873 sharply criticising the Order for its sectarian exuberance. The south Tyrone landlord stated that where Orangeism emerges on estates in Ulster it provokes a counter reaction in extreme nationalism. He sees it as a purely divisive force and he is opposed to it.

A similar figure was Colonel Edward Saunderson who would later become the first leader of Unionism in 1886. Phoenix says that this Liberal MP also took a less than charitable view of the Order at that time. A landlord from County Cavan, whose estate straddled the border, Saunderson 'discouraged Orangeism on his religiously mixed tenancy lands'. He saw the Order as 'bad news because it meant secret combinations, sectarian clashes and trouble in terms of landlord tenant relations.'

The land question was a burning issue all over Ireland in the late nineteenth century, and in the north it divided Presbyterian tenant from Anglican landlord. At the time, the Church of Ireland had all the privileges of the established church in Ireland.

'The Catholics had the chapel, the Presbyterians had their meeting house, and the Anglicans had their rarefied church which was lavish with wealth and patronage by the state,' Phoenix points out, referring to 'the fissures' that this led to between the distant Anglican landlord with a house in Dublin and another estate in England and the poor Presbyterian tenant farmer. The situation caused such tensions that Michael Davitt's Irish National Land League 'actually made inroads into Protestant Ulster in places like Fermanagh and Tyrone'.

The Land League had been formed in 1879 after agitation by Catholic tenant farmers in Mayo and other western counties. In the early 1880s, Land League organisations were established all over Ireland to counter excessive rents charged by landlords and to reform the law to enable every tenant to become owner of his holding by paying a fair rent for a limited number of years. Initially the League cut across sectarian boundaries and some meetings of tenant farmers were held in Orange halls, although a halt was put to this when the landed gentry exerted pressure from within the Orange Order.

The non-conformist Presbyterian tenants who faced rack-renting and evictions were extremely unhappy with their treatment by the landlords. Consequently, the land question made it difficult for people like Saunderson, the Orange Grand Master in the 1870s, to depict himself as leader of all the Protestants of Ulster.

UNIONISM'S SOCIAL CEMENT

The class wounds within the Order were cauterised to an extent by the introduction of Gladstone's 1886 Home Rule Bill for Ireland. It was a clarion call for Protestants and it was a recruiting sergeant for the Orange Institution. 'When Home Rule becomes the emotive force in Anglo-Irish politics, landed gentry like Saunderson and Montgomery change tack as Orangeism emerges as the social cement of unionism,' says Eamon Phoenix. Orangeism brought together 'the master and the man, the landed classes and the middle classes, the shipyard workers and the agricultural labourers'.

Prior to this, Orangeism had had a very Anglican focus, but

now it became 'a blend of denominations in defence of the union'. 'The gentry and the middle classes return to the Orange banner,' Phoenix explains.

They'd been there pragmatically just under a century earlier to oppose the 1798 rising. They'd organised the Orangemen in local yeomanry to curb the United Irishmen. They then withdrew in the 1820s after Orangeism was condemned by the British establishment and regarded the institution as full of bigotry and proletarian expression. Orangeism in the 1840s prior to the Home Rule issue is described by most historians as a working man's drinking club.

Not surprisingly the Orange Institution was against breaking the links with the rest of the United Kingdom and it brought its considerable influence to bear in opposing the Bill. In February 1886, Lord Randolph Churchill was the main speaker at a mass gathering at the Ulster Hall in Belfast. Churchill spoke against Home Rule and was loudly applauded when he used the now-familiar slogan, 'Ulster will fight, and Ulster will be right!'

The first Home Rule Bill was defeated on its second reading by 343 votes to 313. This was followed by the dissolution of the British Parliament and much rejoicing in unionist communities, with the lighting of bonfires on hillsides around Belfast.

Gladstone's second Home Rule Bill in 1893 did get through the House of Commons with the support of nationalist MPs from the Irish Parliamentary Party, but it was defeated in the House of Lords. Phoenix sees as inevitable the defeat of the Bill in the Lords, 'which was the ultimate bulwark against such legislation. The Tories had mastery of the Lords because by tradition it was a Conservative institution.'

The unionists could now 'sit back and ensure their machinery was well oiled so that if another Home Rule crisis came about they would be able to mobilise the Conservatives and Ulster Orangeism to overcome it,' says Phoenix. 'When it comes to mobilisation in the late nineteenth and early twentieth century, everything is revitalised through Orangeism. All the levers of power pass through the Order.'

Gladstone's Liberal government was replaced by the Conservatives, which was good news for Orangemen as the Tories were pro-union. The political respite was short-lived, however, and by 1892 the Liberals were back in power. This time the Orange Order aligned itself with the newly formed Unionist Clubs and, with support from the Conservatives at Westminster, the Bill was defeated.

THE ULSTER PARTY

The Ulster Party was formed in the House of Commons under the leadership of Colonel Edward Saunderson. This party, along with the Ulster Conservative MPs and a few Dublin allies, formed 'the nucleus of the Ulster Unionist Party of decades later' says Phoenix. 'The fact that the Tory party hitched the Ulster anti-Home Rule cause to their Imperial and Conservative banner is very important. By the late 1880s to 1890s you have respectable figures within British politics identifying with Orangeism.'

THE ORANGE SPLIT

With two Home Rule knockouts under its belt and a drawing together of the various strands of Unionism, Orangeism looked to be in a healthy state. Just below the surface, however, dissension was bubbling in the ranks. It exploded to the surface at the 1902 Twelfth demonstration at Castlereagh on the outskirts of east Belfast. The County Grand Master of Belfast, Westminster MP Colonel Edward Saunderson, was publicly challenged and held to account by prominent Belfast socialist and Orangeman Thomas Sloan. Saunderson had pride of place on the speaker's platform, and Sloan, who was also a member of the Belfast Protestant Association, rounded on him, accusing him of voting against the inspection of Catholic convent laundries. Some contend that Sloan's information was wrong, but the damage was done. The most senior Orangeman in Belfast had been heckled and ridiculed in front of his own brethren, and Sloan paid the price by being expelled from the Order. Thomas Sloan, along with some other dissident members, went on to form the Independent Orange Order, marking the first major fracturing of the Orange fraternity.

HOME RULE LOOMS AGAIN

When the Liberals won a landslide victory at the General Election in 1905, unionists knew that Home Rule was back on the political agenda. Over the next five years, while the various strands of unionism in Ireland and Great Britain jockeyed for position in opposing moves towards Home Rule, the Orange Order was never far away.

Meanwhile, at Westminster, the Liberal Party had been reluctant to get involved in the Irish question because it was not popular among the electorate. Then in 1909, the House of Lords went one step too far by blocking Chancellor Lloyd

George's budget proposals. It was the first time in British constitutional history that the Lords had blocked a money bill, and Prime Minister Asquith decided that it was time to 'go to war', as Eamon Phoenix explains:

> In 1911 Asquith introduces the Parliament Act which meant that the House of Lords lost its absolute veto over legislation. The teeth of the Upper House had been drawn and it could no longer block Home Rule; it could only delay it by up to two years. The unionists realised that their greatest barrier at Westminster against Home Rule had been removed.

A siege mentality was growing within the Protestant community. While Protestants were in the majority in the northern counties, they knew that they were the minority within Ireland and they feared betrayal by Westminster and being subjected to Catholic majority rule on the island.

This Protestant paranoia was fuelled by an incident which took place in County Antrim just as the Home Rule crisis was breaking. A mixed marriage involving a Catholic man and a Protestant woman was about to give the unionist/Orange campaign against Home Rule an unexpected propaganda weapon. The 1908 *Ne Temere* Decree by the Catholic Church meant that all children of a mixed marriage had to be baptised and raised as Catholics. Prior to this, many couples compromised by raising male offspring in the father's faith and bringing up girls in the religion of the mother. The Women's Orange Order had been to the forefront of those challenging the Catholic Decree.

This particular family's plight was seized upon by unionists and the Orange Order as proof that their fears of Catholic subjugation were well founded.

Alexander McCann was a Catholic from Ballymena who had married his wife in the Presbyterian church in the early 1890s. In 1910, two years after the *Ne Temere* decree, he absconded with his children, claiming that the Catholic priest had instructed him to do so. As a result, he became what Eamon Phoenix terms 'the greatest asset to Ulster unionists since King Billy'. Pamphlets were published and speeches made, calling for the man's arrest and for the return of the children to their mother. Claims were made that such behaviour was rife throughout Ireland, encouraged by Catholic priests. As Phoenix points out, this was happening at the worst possible time for Irish nationalists – the eve of the Home Rule crisis. For the same reason, it could not have come at a better time from the Ulster unionist/Orange perspective. Mr McCann and his children disappeared without trace and his wife was finally granted a divorce in 1944.

In December 1911, the Ulster area of the Orange Institution created its own temporary Grand Lodge. The Orangemen effectively set up a new headquarters, not in predominantly Catholic Dublin, but in the mainly Protestant and 'loyal' northern counties of Ireland. One of the leading office bearers in the 'Ulster Lodge' was Colonel RH Wallace. He was later to be instrumental in setting up the Ulster Volunteer Force – the forerunner of the ruthless loyalist paramilitary grouping, the UVF. Wallace established an association between the Orange Order and the original UVF which exists to this day.

On Easter Tuesday 1912, a mass rally was held at the Balmoral showgrounds in south Belfast when two hundred thousand people took to the field in a demonstration to the rest of Ireland, Great Britain and the world that 'Ulster loyalists' would not countenance a break in the Union. Members of Parliament, Protestant church leaders, Ulster Clubs members and thousands of Orangemen were among those on parade at Balmoral.

An Ulster Covenant opposing Home Rule was called for and a series of rallies was held across the northern counties to mobilise support. These culminated in an eve of Ulster Day rally at the Ulster Hall in Belfast city centre. Thousands of unionists gathered outside and inside the hall on Bedford Street where Col RH Wallace, Provincial Grand Secretary of the Orange Institution, presented Sir Edward Carson, the Irish Unionist Party leader, with an ancient yellow coloured banner. It was claimed the banner had been carried to victory by the Williamite forces at the Battle of the Boyne in 1690. Carson, a brilliant orator and leading Dublin lawyer, was said to be less than enamoured with some of the Ulster characteristics including the culture of Orangeism. The presentation of the banner on the eve of such a momentus moment in Irish history appeared to have a softening affect and led him to proclaim 'May this flag ever float over a people that can boast of civil and religious liberty!'

The Orange Boyne Standard took pride of place beside the Covenant table in Belfast City Hall the following day when nearly five hundred thousand people signed it on 28 September 1912. Of the 237,368 men who signed, a key percentage were members of the Orange Order.

There was a Covenant for men and there was a parallel Declaration for women. The following is the wording of the document the men signed:

> Being convinced in our consciences that Home Rule would be disastrous to the material well being of Ulster as well as of the whole of Ireland, subversive of our civil and religious freedom, destructive of our citizenship, and perilous to the unity of the Empire, we, whose names are underwritten, men of Ulster, loyal subjects of His Gracious Majesty King George V, humbly relying on the God whom our fathers in days of stress and trial confidently trusted, do hereby pledge ourselves in solemn Covenant throughout this our time of threatened calamity, to stand by one another in defending, for ourselves and our children, our cherished position of equal citizenship in the United Kingdom, and in using all means which may be found necessary to defeat the present conspiracy to set up a Home Rule Parliament in Ireland. And in the event of such a Parliament being forced upon us, we further solemnly and mutually pledge ourselves to refuse to recognise its authority. In sure confidence that God will defend the right, we hereto subscribe our names. And further, we individually declare that we have not already signed this Covenant.

The Declaration for women was less wordy:

> We, whose names are underwritten, women of Ulster and

loyal subjects of our Gracious King, being firmly persuaded that Home Rule would be disastrous to our Country, desire to associate ourselves with the men of Ulster in their uncompromising opposition to the Home Rule Bill now before Parliament, whereby it is proposed to drive Ulster out of her cherished place in the constitution of the United Kingdom, and to place her under the domination and control of a Parliament in Ireland. Praying that from this calamity God will save Ireland, we hereto subscribe our names.

Those not in favour of the union or signing the Ulster Covenant expressed their opinions on the pages of the Belfast newspaper the Irish News. One such person wrote:

At last the curtain has been rung down on the Ulster Day farce, and we may hope for, at any rate, a temporary return to the civic pride on which Belfast prides itself so tremendously. The Carson circus ... gave its final and greatest performance entitled, Signing the Covenant in Belfast on Saturday and wound up its fantastic career in a paroxysm of flag waving and noise, emblematic of the meaningless nonsense of the whole grotesque scheme from start to finish ...

In January 1913, the Ulster Unionist Council – in whose foundation the Orange Order was a driving force – decided that the Volunteers who had been mobilised to resist Home Rule, by whatever means, should become the Ulster Volunteer

Force. These men were to be given firearms training and recruitment was to be limited to those aged between seventeen and sixty-five who had signed the Covenant.

Despite all the rallies, threats and political pressure, on 18 September 1914 the Home Rule Bill got the Royal Assent to become law. In anticipation of this happening, a Provisional Government of Ulster had already been formed, but the preparations for Home Rule were not entirely political. The Ulster Volunteer Force smuggled weapons in from Germany. Gun-running boats made clandestine landings at Larne in County Antrim and Bangor and Donaghadee along the County Down coast. The UVF, with Orangemen swelling its ranks, was readying itself for a showdown with the forces of the Crown if the British government should try to force Ulster into accepting Dublin rule.

The showdown never happened. The outbreak of the First World War of 1914–1918 happened before Home Rule could be implemented. Constitutional change in Ireland was frozen until peace was restored, and 'the loyal sons of Ulster' answered the call to fight for their King and country. The Ulster Volunteer Force, which included Ulster Clubs members and Orangemen, donned the khaki uniforms of the British army, packed their Orange collarettes into their knapsacks and marched off to the Somme to die in Flanders' fields.

The unionist and nationalist leaders in Ireland, Sir Edward Carson and John Redmond, both supported the war effort and urged their followers to join up and fight with the British army. The UVF swelled the ranks of the 36 Ulster Division and members of the Irish Volunteers – a precursor of the IRA – joined the

Irish Brigade within the British forces. Thousands of Orange-men along with members of the Ancient Order of Hibernians (AOH) – the Catholic equivalent of the Orange Order – also enlisted.

In 1998, during the height of the Drumcree protests, a member of the Orange Order and a member of the AOH travelled to a war cemetery in France. Dressed in their respective Orange and Green collarettes, they jointly laid wreaths at the graves of those killed during the Great War. It was a poignant moment which served to remind people that men of both traditions on the island of Ireland had been able to set aside political differences and fight and die together for the common good. The wreath-laying ceremony however, was a long way, both geographically and politically, from the violence and bigotry that was about to be played out yet again on the streets of Northern Ireland.

ORANGE INFLUENCE AT STORMONT

In the post-war period, between 1921 when Ireland was partitioned and 1972 when Stormont was prorogued, virtually every unionist member of the new Northern Ireland parliament was an Orangeman. All the prime ministers and virtually all the cabinet ministers were members of the Order.

Jonathan Mattison of the Orange Order's Education Committee says that this is not as shocking as it sounds. According to him, all of the Prime Ministers were Orangemen 'because the Order was such an integral part of society here'. He continues,

We can't second guess if these politicians would have

risen to the post of premier if they had not been members of the Order. However, given that there was such a large integration of Orangeism in Northern Ireland life, the Orange political support would have been particularly significant.

Some historians believe that without Orangeism there would not have been a separate Northern Ireland state in 1921. When it was established, Orange influence over the unionist government at Stormont was totally disproportionate to the wealth and social standing of the majority of its members. There are examples of working class Orange lodges calling Stormont cabinet ministers to meetings in Orange halls, to raise certain issues with them face-to-face.

Eamon Phoenix has studied the government papers from that period at Stormont, and cites an instance in 1949 when Lieutenant-Colonel Samuel Hall-Thompson, then Minister for Education at Stormont, was summoned to Sandy Row Orange hall to explain why he was increasing grants to Catholic schools. When his reply was unsatisfactory to the lodge members, he was replaced. Ministers and Prime Ministers felt that they were accountable to Orangeism and some, such as Craig and Andrews, were keen to speak at Orange demonstrations and meetings. Phoenix notes that most of the unfortunate sectarian speeches on the Protestant side, from the 1930s onwards, were made at Orange events, with the result that in the minds of nationalists, 'Orangeism became associated with sectarianism and the manipulation of the unionist governments.'

From the end of the war to the early 1970s, sectarianism and dissent festered within the divided community of Northern Ireland as a result of what Catholics saw as unfair Orange influence over the government. This eventually led to a political upheaval heralding the end of unionist-dominated devolved power. When Stormont was prorogued in 1972 and direct rule was established, the levers of power slipped from the hands of Orangeism but, as in previous times of crisis in Ireland, the Order was the mobilising force in a campaign to restore unionism to what Orangemen saw as its rightful place, while providing a bulwark against the growing power of republicanism.

CHAPTER 3

ORANGE RITUAL, STRUCTURES AND MEMBERSHIP

Looking into the Orange Order from outside can be like peering through a dirty window on foggy day. The membership is highly visible through the institution's public parades, its meeting halls are clearly marked and usually prominent buildings, but much of what goes on behind the closed doors of a lodge room is shrouded in mystery, compounded by an ancient ritual cloaked in secrecy. The uninitiated seeking to discover what Orangemen actually do during their meetings have, down through the decades, been mischievously and at other times more cynically, led up the garden path. Folklore and whispered explanations of the ritual have helped to perpetuate the myth of Orangeism. Lodge ceremonies rely heavily on the degrees of Freemasonry, which predate the Orange Order. The Masonic Order – which does not preclude Catholics or other non-conformists to the reformed Protestant faith – has also been the target of finger-pointers for its secret ceremonies, passwords and handshakes. In reality the mass perceptions of

Orange ritual are based more on hearsay than on fact and these are viewed with a level of amusement by those who don't feel threatened by the Order but with suspicion by its detractors.

A popular misconception concerns the practice referred to as 'riding the goat.' Stories have been told of tethered goats being led into Orange halls on meeting nights and brethren gambolling around the lodge room like amateur night at the local rodeo. No Orangeman I have spoken to has ever been at a lodge meeting when a live goat, even one called 'Billy', was introduced to the proceedings. One explanation of the 'goat' story is derived from a very early Masonic ritual book, in which God is referred to as 'God of all things', hence the acronym G.O.A.T. This was subsequently changed so that God was referred to as the 'Great architect of the universe'. There is no doubt that the 'goat' is derived from initialism, but it also has a symbolism stretching back to the middle ages linking it with Satanism. This suited those opposed to such secretive fraternities who used the satanic element to attack the organisations. Proponents of Orange ritual stress their symbolism is a million miles away from that of the devil.

While the precise nature of the ritual alluded to as 'riding the goat' is difficult to pinpoint, members of the Order willing to comment have indicated that it has more to do with a candidate being 'roughed up' during a particular initiation ceremony than being in close proximity to a cloven-hoofed beast. The ritual is understood to be based on a biblical character who undergoes a number of trials during a journey through the wilderness. The ultimate trial involves being 'tossed' between heaven and earth.

During the conferring of degrees in the Royal Arch Purple Order, there is documentary evidence to show that over the years some brethren were injured during the ceremonies. The most serious incident happened in 1925 during a lodge meeting in Newry in County Down. A History of the Royal Arch Purple Order, compiled by the organisations Research Group, refers to a report in a Protestant Truth Society publication about a candidate being shot dead during the conferring of a degree. Lodge members armed with weapons such as a sword, a pike or starting pistol take part in one of the ceremonies to symbolically remind the candidate of the hostile reaction he might face from his fellow brethren if he was to reveal any of the ritual secrets pertaining to that degree. On this occasion, the gun was accidentally loaded with a live round. When the trigger was pulled, the man was shot and fatally wounded. The member responsible for firing the gun was charged and sent for trial but he was eventually acquitted of culpable homicide.

Other candidates were injured during degree ceremonies when some Orangemen carried the inferred physical nature of some initiation rites, too far. Eventually this led to expressions of concern from clergy and doctors who were members of the Order. Discipline and responsibility for the conferring of degrees were tightened up as a result, and the unnecessary suffering of candidates was outlawed.

When questioned about the veracity of these types of allegations, some Orangemen smile knowingly, while others deliberately and mischievously play along with the notion in an attempt, perhaps, to muddy the waters and therefore increase the aura of mystique about the organisation. Most Orangemen say that the majority of the stories are unfounded rumour and treat them with disdain, while doing their best to dispel them. As with any fraternal organisation that is more than two hundred years old, ritual is a part of it, even though it may seem, at the very least, strange, and, at best, outrageously archaic. From the Orange family's standpoint it is historically symbolic and significant and an important element of the workings of a lodge.

THE THREE DEGREES

In its early years, from 1795 to 1798, there were three levels of membership within the Orange Institution. The first and entry level was known as the 'Orange degree'. This was followed by the 'Orange Marksman' degree and then came the 'Purple Marksman' degree. Originally modelled on the degrees of Freemasonry, they were cluttered with ritual and elaborate ceremony.

Most organisations forming at the end of the eighteenth century looked to 'best practice' from already established groups. The Freemasons fell firmly into that category. Jonathan Mattison continues: 'When the rules of the Orange Institution were thrashed out in its early years, you can see in terms of degree structure, it's similar to the Masons. However, there are different meanings, different symbols, and a difference in emphasis compared to Freemasonry.'

When the Grand Orange Lodge was formed in 1798, it sought to streamline the degree structure and put tighter controls on the degrees. The leadership felt that there were too many degrees and too much ritual and it was eventually decided to scrap three of the original Orange degrees. Some members were reluctant to let them go and many lodges still continued the 'illegal' degree work. Eventually the 'illegal three' were merged into one. This became known as the Royal Arch Purple degree and, for the next hundred years, it was looked upon with equal abhorrence by Grand Lodge.

By the early 1900s, a proposal to accept the Royal Arch Purple degree into the Orange Institution of Ireland was put before Grand Lodge. It got two readings by the Orange hierarchy but when it came before a Grand Lodge meeting in Dublin in December 1909 it was rejected.

Mattison outlines the levels of Orangeism that exist today:

> The Orange Institution in Ireland has only two degrees or levels within it. These are the plain Orange and the plain Purple. To the general public everything gets labelled as Orange but there is a clear definition between these two levels within the Orange Institution and another organisation called the Royal Arch Purple Order. In Ireland the Royal Arch is separate from the Orange Institution with one caveat. To be a member of the Royal Arch Purple Order you must first be an Orangeman. And to be a member of the Royal Black Institution you must first be a member of the Royal Arch Purple Order. Despite their separateness, however, all three organisations are regarded as members of what's called the Orange family.

In *The Orange Order: An Evangelical Perspective*, the Rev. Ian Meredith, who was the Grand Chaplain of the Grand Lodge of Scotland, and the Rev. Brian Kennaway, who was the Deputy Grand Chaplain of the Grand Lodge of Ireland, outlined as far as they could the ritual and ceremony of Orange degrees:

> An Orange Lodge meeting ... is marked by the absence of much ritual. There is only the minimum necessary for decorum and to identify valid members. An Orange Lodge meeting consists of prayers, hymns, Bible reading, with explanation or address. The minutes of the previous meeting are read and there is discussion on matters regarding the lodge in particular and Protestantism in general. A new member is escorted into the lodge, takes an obligation of loyalty to his Sovereign, promises that he will uphold the Protestant faith, hears a short lecture on the biblical and historical aspects of Orangeism and takes his place in the lodge. This is known as the first or Orange Degree.
>
> The second Degree is the Purple. It is similar to the Orange Degree; it consists mainly of further lectures on what the Orange Order stands for. There is no esoteric knowledge imparted and ceremonies are full of quotations from the New Testament.
>
> The third Degree in Orangeism is the Royal Arch Purple, which is actually an Order within an Order. In Scotland and England the Purple Order is part of the Orange lodge, while in Ireland it is a separate organisation ... this is the most Masonic-like part of our ceremony. However it is fundamentally different and not Masonic in its theology ... the Degrees of Freemasonry draw on Biblical narratives

and moral teaching but would also add non-Biblical mythology known as traditional history. The Royal Arch Purple Degree is based on Scripture, with no mythology or non-Biblical material. It is a ceremony of instruction with an emphasis on the pilgrimage through life, death, judgement and eternity. For many it is a very moving experience, impressing a sense of eternity and the life of faith in Christ....

To us in the Orange Order the symbols we use simply remind us of well-known Biblical passages and encourage us to think about life, death and the future.... If the Order was stripped of all its ritual, it could continue to exist. Ritual is not basic to its principles and motivation.

ORANGE SYMBOLS

The Orange Order was an amalgam of a number of separate groups that existed in that period, among them the Boyne Societies and the Military Clubs, which already had their own rules and emblems. Historic Orange documents are covered in a multitude of symbols, all with religious or cultural connotations

The Orange Order can claim only six official symbols; however, the Royal Arch Purple Order has many more.

Jonathan Mattison tells of 'a protracted and heated debate' within the Orange Institution which lasted from its foundation until the mid or late nineteenth century. The debate concerned the official symbols of the Order,

The gentry and some of the upper-middle classes didn't

like this throwback to mystical or Freemasonry type elements. This was quite ironic in a way because a lot of the gentry were probably Freemasons themselves and the Orange would have been regarded at that time as a sort of poor man's Masonic.

He says that there was also a feeling that too much symbolism and ritual would draw the attention of the government, which might be looking for reasons to outlaw the organisation. 'The introduction of new legislation also chipped away at the Institution and that is why today we only have six official symbols within the Orange Order.'

The six official Orange symbols, which are worn by brethren on their collarettes and can be seen adorning Orange arches and degree certificates, are: the Holy Bible, symbolising the religious aspect of the Order; the Crown, which is representative of the constitutional settlement of 1688 – as long as the monarchy remains Protestant, that is where the Order's allegiance will lie; Aaron's Rod, symbolising the power of God; the Ark of the Covenant, symbolising the covenant between God and man; the Sword of the Lord and Gideon, which is also a religious symbol; and finally King William, denoting victory at the Battle of the Boyne.

THE INITIATION

Having been initiated into the Orange Order, a candidate is then read the following charge in the lodge room:

Brother, you have been initiated into the Orange

Institution and we now proceed to give you a little of the history of our noble order and its workings. Orange associations were formed in England in 1688 to advance the interests of William III, Prince of Orange. In whose name we associate, whose memory we cherish and who on the 1st July 1690 on the banks of the Boyne defeated the combined forces of Popery and tyranny in this country.

After the battle of the Diamond in 1795, the order was reorganised and formed into Lodges, for the Defence of Protestantism, and for the mutual defence, support and protection of Irish Protestants.

Since then it has had an abiding place in our midst.

This lodge meets on the 1st _____ of the month at the hour of 8 p.m. unless otherwise ordered. At the appointed time the Worshipful Master will call the assembled brethren to attention. After some preliminaries the brethren will form a hand-clasped circle, symbolical of the fraternal ties, which bind Orangemen the world over.

The brethren will thus stand to order while the opening prayer and portion of scripture is being read. After which the Worshipful Master will declare the lodge open and proceed to business. Should you wish to address the lodge, you will rise to your feet, place your right hand over your heart, bow to the occupant of the chair and say Worshipful Master, Deputy Master and Brethren. By placing your hand over your heart you recall the solemn promises you have made. And by bowing to the Worshipful Master you acknowledge his authority which is held from the Grand Orange Lodge of Ireland.

This courtesy must be observed before and after speaking. Should you fail to render it, it is the duty of Deputy Master to call you to order and direct you to salute the chair. Should the lodge be sitting when you arrive you will give your name to the outside Tyler who will pass it inside, and on permission being given to enter, having clothed yourself in the regalia you are entitled to wear, step in front of the Deputy Master's chair, salute the Worshipful Master by the sign of fidelity, bow to the Deputy Master and take your seat.

When visiting another lodge you will give your name and number of your lodge, and on being admitted will adopt the same procedure. Should you wish to leave the lodge before it closes you will rise to your feet, salute the chair, and say, 'Worshipful Master I beg leave to retire.' During the conduct of the business of the lodge you cannot dispute the ruling of the Worshipful Master but should you feel aggrieved you may bring the matter under the notice of the next superior lodge in conformity with the law.

Brother, these are the main points of lodge courtesy, but it is only by constant attendance and by studying our laws, ordinance and customs, also by closely observing the conduct of your seniors in the order that you can acquire a knowledge of all that is required of an Orangeman.

Let me impress upon you the solemn promises you have made, promises which we take as being as binding upon you as an obligation. You have promised you will be true and faithful to every brother Orangeman in all just actions and never know him to be wronged without giving him due notice thereof.

We can all realise what it means to be true and faithful, let these be not mere phrases or words. Help and support your brother Orangeman in preference to those outside the order, and if you know of any injury that is likely to happen to him or if the tongue of slander is busy concerning him it is your bounding duty to acquaint him at once of the circumstances. You have promised never to reveal any of the proceeding of your brother Orangemen in lodge assembled except under certain conditions, and never to attend any act or ceremony of popish worship. These are matters upon which we look seriously and if indulged in may cause your expulsion from our order.

The annual password is taken from the Bible and no member of the order is entitled to it unless he has paid all dues and is in active membership in the lodge. It originates with the Imperial Grand Orange Council of the world and is the same in every part of the world.

When an Orangemen reaches the second or Plain Purple Degree level, a similar charge is read to him.

ROYAL ARCH PURPLE

The next step up in Orangeism is the Royal Arch Purple Degree, which is a separate Order within the Orange Institution. It is the bridge over which candidates cross when moving from the Orange into the Black.

During the formative years of Orangeism there were several changes and revisions of the degrees conferred on the membership. The ritual, which included the original two Orange degrees, was expanded in the early part of 1797 to include the third or Purple Marksman degree.

The *Standard Orange Songbook* contains 'The Marksman's Song'. It outlines in verse the biblical stories upon which those three early degrees were based. The song's first verse gives some indication of this:

Come all my worthy Brethren
That travel this globe around,
Come list awhile 'til I relate
How our Order it was found.
Many is the weary step we travell'd
The wilderness all round.
Till we found the Royal Mark
That led to the Holy Ground.

By the early part of the nineteenth century, a new system of degrees was being devised, with a committee appointed to reduce the initiation ritual of the Purple. Those brethren who treasured the older traditions were concerned at the simplification of the plain Orange and plain Purple degrees. They concluded that there was still room for a third degree but that it must include as much of the ritual of the original three degrees as possible. The Purple Marksman's degree became the Royal Arch Purple Marksman's degree. The term Royal referred to the 'Royal priesthood' from the Bible, with the word Arch meaning chief, as in Archbishop.

Despite warnings of sanction or expulsion by the Grand

Orange Lodge of Ireland, some lodges continued to dabble in degrees, no longer recognised by the Order's hierarchy. The Royal Arch Purple Research Group published a *History of the Royal Arch Purple Order*, which included the following resolution passed by Grand Lodge sometime in 1811–12:

> It having been reported that in defiance of the Rules ... some Masters of Lodges ... have initiated Orangemen into systems which they term Black, Scarlet, Blue, Royal Arch Purple etc... Grand Lodge does acknowledge no other colours or degrees amongst Orangemen but Orange and Purple. Any other colours are illegal and injurious to the true Orange system and if any Orangeman shall presume, after public notice of this resolution to meet in any such Black or other similar lodges, upon due proof thereof he shall be expelled and his name sent to every lodge in the Kingdom.

In 1820, a second 'new system' was introduced. All membership of what was then the Royal Arch Purple Order was declared null and void, with Orangemen having to be re-elected and re-initiated into the new approved Purple Order.

As well as a restructured initiation ceremony, there were new signs and passwords to be learnt.

A meeting was called at the home of John Brown in Scotch Street, Armagh, on 10 July 1820, to discuss the preservation of the 'original Orange Institution'. It was clear from the letter of invitation to this meeting that the discussion would centre on maintaining the Royal Arch Purple Order and as much of its original degrees as possible. It was decided that the Royal Arch would 'shadow' the Orange where possible, with meetings held prior to or immediately after the Orange lodge meetings. This worked only in areas where the Orange brethren existed in large numbers. In Cork and Bandon, in the far south of Ireland, where the membership was smaller, one Royal Arch Purple lodge was established to confer degrees for the entire Orange district. It appears that the Royal Arch lodges existed 'quietly' at a time when they were suffering under the repressive structures put in place by the Grand Orange Lodge of Ireland. The Royal Arch men kept their heads well below the parapets as numerous attempts were made to force this Order within an Order into oblivion.

When the Grand Orange Lodges of Ireland and Great Britain both dissolved in 1836, a ten-year period of uncertainty followed, when a variety of Loyal Order 'systems' were put to the test. The colourful array of brethren at that time was also tested. They included: Orangemen, Purplemen, Marksmen, Bluemen, Scarletmen, Brownmen, Whitemen, Golden Garter, Red Cross and Flaming Sword men.

The Royal Arch was torn between two Orders during this period: the Orange and the Black. Contemporary records show that it dallied with both. Eventually the 'made' men decided to establish their own independent institution. The inaugural meeting of the Grand Royal Arch Purple Chapter of Ireland was held on 30 November 1911 at Clifton Street Orange Hall in north Belfast. The minutes from that meeting recorded 1,420 Royal Arch chapters in Ireland, from Londonderry to Longford, from Cavan to Cork and from Dublin to Donegal.

ROYAL ARCH EMBLEMS AND SYMBOLS

The emblems and symbols of the Royal Arch Purple degree are numerous, varied and, to the uninitiated eye, confusing. The Holy Bible shows from where the teachings of the Order are derived. The Ark of the Covenant is evidence of God's promise to guide his people to safety. The Anchor is symbolic of a safe arrival after the stormy voyage through life. The Ladder has its three steps of Faith, Hope and Charity. The Five-Pointed Star, or Pentalpha, represents fellowship and dependency. The Coffin is a reminder of the mortality of mankind. The Three-Branched Candlestick is a reminder of the Holy Trinity. The Arch indicates strength and durability. Finally, the Sword pointing to the heart is a reminder of the hostile reception endured by a candidate until it was proven that his intentions were serious and friendly.

The hallmark of the Royal Arch Purple Order is considered to be the number two and a half. The number is biblically based and featured in a part of the ancient ritual:

Question: What are you?

Answer: A true Israelite.

Question: Who are you?

Answer: One of the elect.

Question: How do you know that?

Answer: By a true sign and token.

Question: What is your token?

Answer: The rod of Aaron.

Question: Why?

Answer: Because it was laid up as a signal or token

	against the rebels.
Question:	The password?
Answer:	Gideon.
Question:	What is your number?
Answer:	Two and a half.
Question:	What two and a half?
Answer:	The tribe of Reuben, the tribe of Gad and the half tribe of Manasseh.
Question:	The main password?
Answer:	Hallelujah.
Question:	Why is Hallelujah your password?
Answer:	Because it was an elect word and we are an elect people.

STRUCTURE OF THE LOYAL ORANGE INSTITUTION

All Loyal Order structures are similar and are derived from those of the Loyal Orange Institution. The Orange Order in Ireland is built like a pyramid. At its foundation are the 1,400 private Orange lodges, providing the localised 'power-base' of the institution. Above these are the 125 District Orange lodges drawn from specific geographical areas. These District lodges comprise representatives of every private lodge in that area. The next level consists of a dozen County Grand Lodges – Antrim, Armagh, Belfast, Down, Londonderry, city of Londonderry, Tyrone, Fermanagh, Cavan, Donegal, Leitrim and Monaghan. The County lodge membership is drawn from the various District lodges. At the apex of the pyramid is the Grand Lodge of Ireland. It has three hundred members drawn from all the County Grand Lodges plus a representative from each District lodge. Presiding over the Grand Lodge of Ireland is the Grand Master.

The word of Grand Lodge and the Grand Master is supposed to be final, but historically this hasn't always been the case. For over two hundred years, the grassroots members of the Order have at times ignored or openly defied Grand Lodge rulings. Many Orangemen sitting on the foundation stones would argue that it is not a democratic organisation while there are those at the top level who would contend that the institution is too democratic for its own good.

The Order has its fault lines but despite being shaken to the core at various points over the last two centuries, it hasn't crumbled and fallen as many people predicted. Neil Jarman of the Institute for Conflict Research says that this is no mean achievement and he believes that there is a fundamental rationale behind it:

I think the Order is probably the one organisation in Northern Ireland that's held the Unionist/Protestant community together to an extent. It remained open and accessible to all shades of political opinion within that community. You had members of the UDA and UVF within the organisation along with key political figures including members of Parliament and senior party figures. There were also various shades of religious opinion. The only real schism was during the battle for independence in Ireland in the early twentieth century.

The comparison is also made with the bitter and sometimes

fatal infighting that existed between the politicians, the para-militaries and the churches in the Protestant community during the Troubles and the relative togetherness of the Orange Order. The Twelfth of July is still the one occasion annually when, according to Jarman, all the prods come out to redefine themselves in their own terms:

> Because it's such an inclusive event, we've seen the Orangemen allowing the UVF bands and UDA bands to be there. Looking in from the outside, that can be perceived as very problematic and the Order has been criticised for it, but within the rationale of the Orange being a broad church for the unionist community it's had to do it and that's helped to sustain the whole process over the last thirty years.

There are those at the highest level within the Orange Order who believe that the time has come for changes in some of the archaic structures of the institution. Equally there are also many members who recoil instantly at talk of change. They see the structure, ritual, symbolism and ceremony as prized ingredients of the Orange culture, and believe that brethren should tinker with them at their peril. There is a view that 'what was good enough for my great grandfather's lodge in his day is good enough for me and my lodge today.'

THE ROYAL BLACK INSTITUTION

The Royal Black Institution could be described as the 'regular church-attending big brother' of the Orange Institution.

The Black, as it is more commonly known, was formed in 1797, two years after the Orange. Its origins lie also in County Armagh and it grew out of a desire by men seeking a more religion-based fraternity, one step removed from the more defence-oriented nature of the Orange. Many of those involved in bringing this about were already members of the newly formed Orange Institution and the existing Masonic Order in Ireland. The latter influenced the adoption of certain emblems and symbols in those formative years. Some Masonic-style symbols are still clearly visible today on the black collarettes and navy blue velvet aprons worn by members of the Royal Black Institution on parade. While members of the Masonic Order are undoubtedly members of the Black today, the Institution says that there is no longer any formal Masonic connection, only a resemblance.

On 14 September 1846, a meeting took place in Portadown, formalising the structure and organisation of the Royal Black Institution. This reconstitution created for the new Order a more permanent, inspirational and disciplined template which exists to this day.

The structure of the Black institution is tiered like that of the Orange. The foundation stones are the local lodges known as *preceptories*. Like the Orange lodges, each Royal Black preceptory is issued with a unique number when the institution's governing body grants it a warrant. This is effectively a licence to exist. Each preceptory elects officers, and they represent the members at the next tier – the District Chapter. Officers from the District chapters together form a County or Provincial Grand Chapter. The officers from the various County or

Provincial chapters make up the institution's governing body which is known as the Imperial Grand Council. The Council determines the rules and regulations of the order worldwide and is recognised by all members of the Imperial Grand Black Chapter of the British Commonwealth, which is another name for the Royal Black Institution itself. The Commonwealth title, although not commonly used, can be found inscribed on all warrants, certificates and official correspondence used by the Black.

You cannot be a Blackman unless you are an Orangeman. This seemingly contradictory statement is nevertheless true. To become a member of the Royal Black Institution, you must first be a member of the Orange Order. A vetting process takes place and Orangemen are approached and invited to join the Black. This link was formalised only in the late 1800s, after much squabbling amongst the Protestant fraternities that existed at that time. Records from that period are scarce but it seems that the leaders of the Orange and Black recognised that it was better for both organisations if they established a 'rite of passage' between the two Orders, thus bringing an end to the bickering. That rite of passage, however, meant travelling through another Order within the Orange family, the Royal Arch Purple.

There are a number of Blackmen who would gladly relinquish the link with the Orange if they could retain their membership of the RBI because of the bad publicity attached it has garnered in recent years. While they have discussed such a move amongst themselves, it is not a subject of formal debate at any level within the loyal Orders. Historically there has been a level of antipathy towards the Black by certain members of the Orange as seen during the 1800s when controversy raged over what some saw as the unnecessarily high number of loyal Orders being created at that time. There are distinct differences between the Black and the Orange. While the Orange Order has the British Monarch at the very heart of its proceedings, the Black Institution has the Holy Bible. The Orange took its colour from the Dutch King William at the Battle of the Boyne. So why did the other institution settle on Black? The answer can be found in the Bible, with Black being the colour of mourning. This serves to remind each member of his own mortality. The Royal prefix of the Black Institution has nothing to do with the British monarch or the House of Windsor. It too is Bible based, arising from the scriptures pertaining to the 'royal priesthood of Israel'.

Exodus 19: 5–6 'Now therefore, if you will obey my voice indeed and keep my covenant, then you shall be a peculiar treasure unto me above all people: for all the earth is mine: And you shall be unto me a kingdom of priests, and a holy nation....'

1 Peter 2: 9 '...But ye are a chosen generation, a royal priesthood, a holy nation, a peculiar people; that you should show forth the praises of him who has called you out of darkness into marvellous light.'

The principal emblem of the Royal Black Institution is the Red Cross which is drawn from the biblical story of Jesus being crucified and then rising again from the dead.

The current Sovereign Grand Master of the Royal Black Institution, William Logan, says, 'While being aware of our own mortality as symbolised by the colour black, we are also very aware that other things happen when we depart this life. That there is a survival of the spirit. The afterlife. That's what the Red Cross symbol teaches us, that there is a resurrection.'

While the Orange Order has always had a political dimension within its framework, the Black has not. The Institution's leaders stress that it is an organisation based solely on the scriptures and nothing else. They also contend that the Royal Black Institution is not a marching organisation.

According to William Logan, 'We walk in an orderly procession; we don't march. Furthermore, we are always proceeding to or from a service of Christian worship. All our banners are painted with scenes from the Bible and scriptural writings. The only scenes of violence depicted are those between David and Goliath. There are no pictures of a big man on a white horse.'

Some religious fundamentalists have accused the Black of being 'another church with secretive rituals'. This is flatly denied by the Institution. 'We are auxiliaries to the Christian reformed churches,' says Logan. 'As a worldwide organisation we exist to give our members the opportunity to study the Holy Scripture, increase their knowledge of the reformed faith, engage in Christian and charitable outreach and continue to further develop social and responsible citizenship.'

However, with meetings held behind closed doors, where ancient rituals are enacted, Loyal orders like the Black and Orange leave themselves open to allegations of dark dealings and mischievous goings-on.

'People talk about secrets and mysteries,' says William Logan. 'Yes, there are matters which are confidential to the membership but are open to everybody to interpret if they just read the Bible. Everything to do with the Black can be found in the Holy Bible.'

The average preceptory meeting opens with a prayer, a scripture reading and the singing of a hymn. Much of the other business can be taken up with mundane agenda topics such as reading and approving the minutes of the previous meeting. The treasurer will report on the financial state of the precep- tory. Further down the agenda comes the degree work or level of religious instruction. This can take up to an hour to com- plete. William Logan believes that this speaks volumes for people who want to join and be a regular attendee within the Royal Black Institution.

'There must be something there when you get men coming along on a regular monthly basis to sit and listen to that,' he says. 'There must be something that grips a man, when he is prepared to leave his home and come along to a meeting in a sometimes draughty old country Orange Hall [the majority of Black preceptory meetings are held in Orange Halls]. To sit and listen to men rehearsing Biblical matters.'

After the formal meeting, there's time for the social element. Logan continues, 'In a lot of cases, particularly country halls, when the business is completed and the meeting is called to a close, there's a cup of tea. The sandwiches and biscuits are passed round as the members, some of them puffing on pipes and others smoking a cigarette, sit by the hall fire yarning and talking.'

This may sound somewhat archaic in a modern technologi- cal age but in the days before 24-hour satellite television and all the other distractions that have proliferated from that, this type of fraternal social interaction was the glue that helped to hold some rural Protestant communities together.

'There is nothing in the Institution that's sinister or harmful in any way to anyone or that would offer any sort of offence to anyone,' Logan emphasises. 'The Black's teachings and the emblems that we use all have biblical messages that transmit to our membership the way to lead a better and more fruitful life within the community.'

BLACK EMBLEMS

The following emblems play a part in the ritual associated with the workings of the Royal Black Institution:

The Red Cross signifies the biblical story of Christ crucified on the cross and then rising again from the dead. This symbolises the members' belief in an afterlife.

The Burning Bush refers to the biblical story of Moses hearing the voice of God from the burning bush. He was given instructions by the voice, which he followed to lead the people of Israel out of Egypt. This is the lesson of obedience.

The symbol of the Dove with the Olive Leaf is taken from the biblical story of Noah who was told by God to build an ark before the great flood. When Noah sent the dove out after the rains had stopped, it returned with an olive leaf in its mouth, showing that the waters were abating, the land was returning to normal and Noah and his family had survived. This is also a lesson of obedience.

The Hour Glass signifies that the sands of time are running through for everyone and people have an opportunity to mend their ways to become more acceptable in a Christian sense before meeting their maker.

'None of us is perfect,' says the Sovereign Grand Master. 'We try to live our lives in line with these Christian teachings in so far as we possibly can. The Black tries to instil these values in the membership but we are very aware that we are not paragons of virtue or plaster saints. We've all got frailties and failings.'

With such demanding standards, Logan concedes that it can be difficult to get the right sort of person to join the Black:

> We're living in a modern age now where younger members coming into the Order haven't had the church Sunday School experience that many of the older members had when they were growing up. It could well be that we have people joining the Black who perhaps haven't had any experience of biblical matters before. The first contact they have is when they're on their knee in a Royal Black preceptory meeting room, with their hand on the Holy Bible, ready to take an obligation that they'll try to live up to the standards that the Institution is asking of them.

In light of such recruitment difficulties, it could be assumed that corners would be cut and standards lowered to attract more candidates. The Sovereign Grand Master, however, is adamant that this is not the case. 'You can't just join the Orange Order one day and became a Blackman the next,' he stresses. 'A period of time will pass when a person's suitability to become a member of the Black will be tested.' After that, the prospective member will be invited to join a preceptory. 'Who knows what spark it's going to light? If you repeat the Christian message to people often enough at preceptory meetings, there is no telling what effect it can have on their lives.'

DEGREES OF INSTRUCTION

There are twelve separate degrees or levels within the Royal Black Institution compared to the three degrees that exist within the Orange Institution. Each degree attained by a member represents another level of instruction having been successfully completed. The degree format is described as an intensive question and answer session involving the preceptory candidate watching and listening to more qualified members involved in an inquisitive exchange based on set biblical readings.

'By the time a preceptory member has reached the twelfth, or Red Cross, degree he should have a better understanding of what the Institution is about and what it's trying to do for society and for the individual,' says William Logan.

He explains that there is 'a completely different feeling' about the Royal Black Institution. While all members are also Orangemen, they conduct themselves differently at meetings. 'There is respect for one another, as there is in many areas of Orangeism too, but there's a more reverent atmosphere within a preceptory meeting.'

WORLDWIDE MEMBERSHIP

There are about twenty-five thousand members of the Royal Black Institution worldwide. Up to eighteen thousand of those are in Ireland. The Order can be found in the United Kingdom and the Republic of Ireland, Canada, the United States of America, Australia, New Zealand, South Africa, Togo and Ghana. Like Orangeism, the Black reached these far-flung shores via missionary work and members of the Order who were serving with the British army when the Empire was at its zenith. Similarly the Black Institution feels the knock-on effect of any decrease in the membership of the Orange Order.

Imperial Grand Master William Logan notices the changes in his own preceptory, where in 1950 there were 120 members, whereas now there are fewer than thirty. 'Back then there were tens of thousands of members,' he recalls.

ON PARADE

The Royal Black Institution holds its main procession each year on the last Saturday in August. This day has no historical significance; it does not commemorate a battle or a victory. It was selected because the month of August was traditionally the working man's holiday in towns and cities throughout Ireland, and in the rural areas it was the break for farm labourers before the harvest.

Ideally the preceptory members are required to wear certain regalia on parade and this usually includes a dark suit, a collarette with a carnation flower in it, a Royal Black Institution Apron (Masonic influence), a bowler hat and white gloves. The rolled-up umbrella is an optional extra, depending on the weather. Thousands of Blackmen take to the streets in towns and villages across Northern Ireland on this day, usually at six different venues. Thousands of people, including the families and friends of the members, pack a picnic and turn out to watch the processions. Earlier in the month, on the second Saturday in August, a smaller parade is held in Fermanagh, when local preceptories, along with those from Cavan, Donegal and Monaghan, attend. Scotland has its own gathering for all the Scottish preceptories.

The other annual event organised by the Institution is the sham fight at Scarva on the day after the Twelfth of July demonstrations. The village of Scarva nestles in the rolling hills and drumlins of County Down. Blackmen from Portadown, Newry, Tandragee, Markethill, Banbridge, Rathfriland and Lower Iveagh parade to the annual sham fight. Hundreds of spectators also come along to watch a re-enactment of the Battle of the Boyne. Volunteers dressed in historical costumes and armed with musket, pike and sword engage in a mock Battle, the outcome of which has been known for over three hundred years. This is probably as close as the Royal Black Institution comes, in this modern age, to the violent historical beginnings to which all the Loyal Orders in Ireland can trace their ancestry.

CHARITY

The Royal Black Institution is heavily committed to charity work. Its mission statement includes Christian and charitable outreach and the members take this as seriously as they do developing the influence of the reformed faith. Generations of Blackmen have been involved in fund-raising at local preceptory level, regularly handing over relatively small donations to charities. In recent years, however, the Order's leadership has adopted a more co-ordinated, sustained and substantial fund-raising approach within the Institution. In 2002, £65,000 was given to the Chest, Heart and Stroke Association in Northern Ireland. In 2004, £80,000 was raised for a multiple sclerosis charity; and in 2006, Christian Mission work in central Africa benefited to the tune of £70,000.

THE FUTURE

The Black Institution has been involved in the Joint Loyal Orders Working Group and William Logan has attended many of the meetings with the Catholic hierarchy and nationalist political representatives. '

'Having direct contact with those people means we can learn from each other,' he says.

At this point, however, meeting with republican residents' groups does not appear to be on the cards. 'More forgiveness is needed and more Christian belief is required if we are to meet residents' groups.'

Asked about plans for the future, he replies,

> We need to maintain our relevance in the community in the years ahead. The Ten Commandments need to be defended and we need to draw moral and ethical standards to people's attention. That's our message and it will be relevant for the next two thousand years.'

It's a message that will only be relayed to members of the male population because unlike its sister Order, the Black Institution does not have a female equivalent. While there are Orangewomen, there are no Blackwomen. According to those within the Order, female preceptories simply have not happened and there is no indication that the status quo is going to change.

ORANGEWOMEN AND CHILDREN

Contrary to popular belief, the Women's Loyal Orange Order does not exist to make tea for the Orangemen. It is an organisation in its own right with its own rules and regulations, and is recognised as such by the Orange Institution.

The first female foray into the ranks of Orangeism, however, was a relatively short-lived affair. The Association of Loyal Orangewomen of Ireland was formed in the middle of the nineteenth century, but just over twenty-five years later the movement was mothballed. By the turn of the century, however, wheels were again in motion to reconstitute the Orangewomen's franchise. At the forefront of this fledgling group was Cavan woman Mary Johnstone. A native of Bawnboy and a member of the dormant Association of Orangewomen, she was married to the Senior Deputy Grand Master of Ireland, and this fact undoubtedly helped strengthen her case.

Within a few weeks, Mary Johnstone had called the first meeting of the new Orangewomen's Association. They got together early in the New Year at 12 Rutland Square in Dublin where the first three Women's Order lodge warrants were issued in February 1912. Lodge Warrant No. 1 went to a lodge meeting in Sandy Row Orange Hall in the loyalist heartland of south Belfast. The second went to Ballymacarrett in the east of the city and the third warrant was presented to a lodge from Kingstown (now Dún Laoghaire) in County Dublin.

The male brethren have no jurisdiction over the female

brethren's Association, which is not officially part of the Orange Order. Nevertheless, the women's lodges are closely aligned with those of the men. They are involved in a range of activities, including helping with the restoration and renovation of Orange halls. Most of the Associations' activity however, is of a charitable nature. Collections are taken up for the Orange Benevolent Fund and every year official ceremonies are held when cheques are handed over. While such events never feature in the national press and media, photographs can be found periodically in many local weekly papers.

Grand Mistress Olive Whitten says that the charity collections are a very important part of what the Association is about:

> We've collected £1,000 a year for the past two decades. Some of the money is gathered when a charity box for small change is passed round the room at each lodge meeting. We've donated to Orange charities and outside groups such as the Northern Ireland Hospice, Cancer Research and the Royal National Lifeboat Institution. We raise a lot of money each year and I'd like to think if we're remembered for anything it would be for our charity work.

According to their records, membership increased throughout the twentieth century with Women's Order County lodges being established in Down, Armagh, Antrim, Tyrone, Fermanagh and Londonderry. In the latter part of the 1990s, new women's lodges were opened in Counties Donegal and Monaghan. The Association says that membership in these two counties is still vibrant but the Orangewomen of Cavan and Dublin dwindled and eventually were forced to close and return their warrants. There are two District lodges in London-derry and enough registered lodges elsewhere in Northern Ireland to sustain Women's Order County Grand Lodges in Antrim, Armagh, Belfast, Fermanagh and Tyrone. When the women's Association was flourishing, there were up to seven thousand members in Ireland, but today that figure stands at just under two thousand.

In the men's Order, members are given the title 'Brother' upon entry. In the Women's Loyal Orange Order, the term 'Sister' is used before each member's name. Sister Mary Johnstone from Cavan, held the position of Grand Mistress of the Association of Loyal Orangewomen of Ireland from the outset of the rejuvenation of the Order until 1923. By this time, Ireland had been partitioned and Johnstone's successors have all come from counties north of the border: Sister Leah Garrett from Bangor 1923–1934; Sister Margaret Drennan from Belfast 1934–1968; Sister Elizabeth McCrum, a Justice of the Peace from Belfast 1968–1993; Sister Doreen Williamson from Belfast 1993–1998; Sister Olive Whitten M.B.E. from Armagh 1998 to present day.

WOMEN ON PARADE

In a parade of Orangemen, the appearance of a women's lodge can be an arresting sight. In the past, many women would parade in brightly coloured frocks and hats, in stark contrast to the male brethren's dark suits. The women's policy on suitable attire on parade has been relaxed in recent years, with trouser suits being allowed. The wearing of a hat was never a prerequisite, according to Grand Mistress Olive Whitten,

> It used to be that a skirt or a frock was the order of the day for parades but it was only customary to wear a hat. I can still remember my mother dressing up in her second-best coat, hat and gloves when she went to Portadown on a shopping trip. We like to encourage the women to keep up the standards.

The women's association does not have a marching culture, although it encourages its members to take part in parades to church services and the annual Twelfth demonstrations. The women have no absolute right to parade with their male counterparts, but the Sisters may take part if they receive a written invitation to do so from the lodges that are organising the parades. This in turn has to receive the approval of Women's Grand Lodge.

Orange historian Jonathan Mattison draws a clear demarcation line between the Orangewomen and the Orangemen. 'They are a completely separate entity,' he says. 'They can make a request to join a parade but they must be issued with an invitation before they take part in a demonstration.' In Ireland Orangewomen are not allowed to attend male lodge meetings. However, in Scotland they can attend male lodge meetings if they receive an invitation to do so.

The women don't wear full Orange regalia on parade or in the lodge room. Instead of the traditional Orange sash or collarette, they wear a ribbon-like collarette similar to that worn by the Junior Orange lodges. The Women's Order also has a Junior section but it is facing the same problems over recruitment as the boys' Order. The number of new recruits is few and the candidates are usually daughters following their mothers into the Order.

THE JUVENILES

The youth wing of the men's Orange Order is commonly known as the Juveniles. The Junior Orange Order caters for boys aged between seven and seventeen. There have been Junior lodges operating in Belfast since the 1800s, but these individual lodges were not formalised into an association until after the end of the First World War. An Executive Committee of the Grand Orange Lodge of Ireland was appointed in 1925 to administer the affairs of the Junior Orangemen. However, the growing number of boys joining necessitated another change in 1974 when the running of the Juveniles was handed over to the newly formed Junior Grand Orange Lodge.

The organisation, which now operates under the auspices of the Grand Orange Lodge, has its own rules and structures which are firmly rooted in those of the Orange Institution. When its members reach the age of 18, they are eligible to move into the adult Order. There is an annual parade when all the Junior Orangemen gather at one location. Instead of the full-size Orange collarette or sash, they wear a thin ribbon-like collarette which is similar to that worn by the Women's Orange Order.

The Juvenile section is much smaller numerically than the Orange Institution and it faces the same problems as any other youth group in this modern age. In many instances, the problems mirror those affecting recruitment in the adult Order. The formal trappings of the Junior Orange lodges and the prospect of dressing up in your 'Sunday suit' and wearing a 'skinny sash' is much less attractive to a young boy than the colourful uniforms and 'cool' image represented by the multitude of flute bands on parade.

Institute for Conflict Research Director Neil Jarman says,

> The tradition where people introduce their kids to Orangeism at an early age – literally following in their fathers' footsteps – is a fading tradition. More young people today are joining the loyalist flute bands that march with the lodges. That's probably why a lot of people come out to watch the parades, because of the bands. While some bands are closely associated with paramilitary groups, they do provide a good and important level of local organisation.

The menacing nature of some of these loyalist bands, and particularly the crowds of alcohol-swilling supporters who follow them, can present one of the less attractive elements of a parade. Many Protestants as well as Catholics who find themselves in close proximity to these bands on parade can feel intimidated; complaints from residents about bandsmen and their supporters urinating in the gardens of south Belfast's leafy suburbs during the annual Twelfth demonstration are legion.

According to Jarman, however, there is a plus to be drawn from this unlikely quarter, in the opportunity the bands provide for young people to learn and to play music. 'If you consider how the bands work, the time put into practising, the way the bandsmen teach each other, there is nothing like it anywhere else in the UK,' he says.

In contrast, the Junior Order aims to provide a solid platform from which young people can begin to understand the basic principles of the Reformed Faith and Orangeism. When the comparison is drawn between this and the marching bands, it is easy to understand why some Junior Lodge Superintendents may feel as if they are beating their heads against an empty lodge room wall. The problem of recruitment generally has been a recurring one with the membership going through a series of peaks and troughs but the parades issue was to become at first a recruiting sergeant for the Order before developing into a propaganda disaster that would drive people away from the institution in their droves.

THE TROUBLED TRADITIONAL ROUTES

Northern Ireland's long history of violent atrocities and sectarian conflict claimed thousands of lives as republicans, loyalists and the security forces fought a bitter and bloody war. Virtually every political or security initiative had its own violent aftermath: internment in 1971; the Ulster Workers Council strike in 1974; the republican hunger strike in 1981; and the 1985 Anglo–Irish Agreement were just a few of the milestones on a road stained with blood.

Neil Jarman outlines the part played by parades throughout Irish history:

Parades have been a live issue in Ireland for two hundred years. The first Catholic was killed in a fight connected with an Orange parade in the late 1700s and there have been periods of time, particularly during political turmoil, when parades in Ireland have been highly contentious. You had it around O'Connell's time in the 1830s and you had it through the Home Rule period from the 1870s onwards. When parades bring masses of people out onto the streets and these people get mobilised, they also get politicised.

From its earliest days, parading has been a central tenet of the Orange Order. It has been as important a part of being an Orangeman as the ritual and regalia, the fraternity and the upholding of the reformed faith. Ask many Orangemen why they joined the Order and they will cite parading as one of the primary reasons.

On 12 July 1796, just ten months after the formation of the Loyal Orange Institution, the Order's first Boyne Commemoration Parade took place. This was the forerunner of the present day Twelfth demonstrations which mark the victory of King William of Orange over King James at the River Boyne, not far from Drogheda in County Louth. In broad terms, William was the 'Protestant victor over the Catholic foes'.

The figures vary but it is estimated that James led the Jacobite forces of about 26,000 men while William rode at the head of an army of 36,000 of various nationalities. William, who was also known as the Prince of Orange, set foot on Irish soil at Carrickfergus in County Antrim in June 1690, a few weeks before the Battle of the Boyne. As he marched his army south through Loughbrickland in County Down he was advised by his senior officers, including his second-in-command the Duke of Schomberg, to proceed with caution. William, however, was feeling the pressure from England where discontent was growing over the slowness of the campaign in Ireland. The King is reported to have said at the time that he 'had not come to Ireland to let the grass grow under his feet.' The Jacobite army of Catholic King James retreated before the advancing Williamite forces before finally making a stand on the banks of River Boyne near Drogheda on the Louth/Meath border. William felt the geography of the location bode well for a short and conclusive confrontation because while James held the stronger position, his forces were smaller numerically and regarded as inferior militarily apart from some excellent French infantry and very good Irish cavalry. The Williamite forces included most of the Protestant nations in Europe: the Germans, the Dutch, the Danes and the Finns, all battle-hardened troops. Among the most committed soldiers were the Protestant Huguenots from France who were bent on avenging the barbarous treatment they had suffered during the persecuting policy of the French monarch Louis XIV. Louis was backing James's campaign to regain the throne of England and Scotland with money and men. The 'Sun King' was aiming to extend the dominance of France and her allies across Europe and King William and his supporters, which included the Vatican, were intent to putting a stop to it and securing the Glorious Revolution. William, although wounded, was victorious at the Battle of the Boyne and while the conflict has been viewed simply as a victory for Protestants over Catholics, more recently historians have painted a slightly less sectarian scenario. Both armies were religiously mixed; King William's elite Dutch Blue Guards were predominantly Catholic and they went into battle carrying a papal banner – being part of a cross-Christian alliance to stop the French conquest of Europe.

Casualties for such a momentous battle were comparatively light. It's estimated that five hundred Williamite soldiers died along with 1,500 Jacobites and this is attributed to the fact that William did not immediately pursue the retreating army, which fought a valiant rear guard action. James fled to Dublin with his cavalry escort. He was met at Dublin Castle by Lady Tyrconnell – whose husband had raised an army drawn from throughout Ireland in support of James – and it is reputed that he told her 'Your countrymen, madam, can run well.' Her Ladyship is said to have retorted, 'Not quite so well as your majesty, for I see you have won the race.'

Ironically for an event historically associated with Protestantism, a Pope had a hand in deciding the date on which victory at the Boyne would be commemorated. The actual battle was fought and won on 1 July, but it is celebrated on 12 July because of a change from the Julian to the Gregorian calendar. When this was first decreed by Pope Gregory XIII in 1582, ten days were dropped from the existing Julian calendar. Some countries resisted the change, Britain and Ireland among them. It was further decreed that any country which delayed introducing the Gregorian version beyond AD 1700 should add eleven days. When the British Isles eventually adopted the Gregorian calendar in 1752, 1 July became 12

July, and the rest is history.

A VERY PUBLIC DISPLAY

Parades were viewed by the Orange leadership as 'an appropriate medium to witness for their faith and to celebrate their cultural heritage,' according to the Grand Orange Lodge of Ireland website. It also stresses that parades by Boyne Societies and other similar groups predate the formation of the Orange Order and have traditionally existed within the Protestant community.

Historian Jonathan Mattison outlines the historical significance of parading for Orangemen.

It's been there from day one. The various Boyne Societies, which existed before the Orange Order, marched. In England there is a tradition of walking the parish boundaries once a year. It's an outward celebration and a public display. The first Twelfth Orange parade was in 1796 and we've been celebrating the Glorious Revolution ever since. In the very early days in Londonderry, military units that were stationed there celebrated the lifting of the city's siege with a parade. Similarly in Canada military units in the nineteenth century celebrated the anniversaries of the Williamite wars, so parading became an aspect of popular culture on both sides of the Atlantic.

Those vehemently opposed to Orange parades see them as 'triumphalist' occasions of 'rabble rousing' by 'coat-trailing bigots'. The Order uses different terminology ranging from 'colourful displays of pageantry full of religious, cultural and political symbolism' to a 'commemoration of the Glorious Revolution and all the benefits that flowed from it'. The Order cites the Bill of Rights of 1689, the Triennial Act of 1694 and the 1695 Freedom of the Press Act, which it points out benefited all the people – Catholic and Protestant.

Orange lodges parade in full regalia with flags and banners. The flags are usually the British Union flag, the Northern Ireland or 'Ulster' flag, and the Orange flag which consists of the Cross of St George and a purple star on an orange background. Individual lodges also carry skilfully hand-painted banners depicting biblical stories or historic battle scenes, famous Orangemen and other important events in the story of Orangeism.

A NOTE OF DISCORD

Music is also an important part of any parade. The most traditional musical instruments include the Lambeg drum and the fife. The fife is a small, shrill, whistle-type instrument and the Lambeg is one of the biggest and loudest drums to be carried in a parade anywhere in the world. It is constructed using goat skins stretched over a double head of approximately 93 cm in diameter. The drum is 61 cm wide and weighs about 20 kg. It is carried on the chest using a neck-strap and is played using malacca or bamboo canes.

There are many theories on its origins but the most common is that the Lambeg is derived from the large side-drums brought to Ireland from Holland by the Duke of Schomberg's soldiers who fought with William of Orange at the Battle of the Boyne.

It is also claimed that the Lambeg drum was first played at the Battle of the Diamond in 1795, while others say that the first drum of this kind was not made until much later when it was used in the Twelfth Orange parade in Lambeg in County Antrim in 1870.

Most Orangemen march to the beat of flute, brass, accordion and pipe bands. The musicianship can be of mixed quality, with the best bands putting in hours of practice for months ahead of the marching season. In tiny halls across Northern Ireland, they rehearse their tunes over and over again; youngsters are instructed by older members, and generations of the same family are often present in the bands. Members organise their own fund-raising to pay for their instruments and their colourful uniforms.

Throughout the 1980s and 1990s, there was a proliferation of what became known as 'kick the pope' flute bands. Formed in hard-line loyalist areas, they became a source of recruitment for whole classes of teenagers. In some instances, there have been accusations that such bands are little more than musical fronts for particular loyalist paramilitary groups. With their music heavily reliant on a core of drummers accompanied by shrill flutes, another moniker alludes to 'blood and thunder' bands, so called because of the volume they manage to generate and the lyrics associated with their repertoire. They often play what have become known as 'party tunes' – music guaranteed to prompt its listeners to some visceral reaction. Regular favourites – indeed nationalist critics would contend their only tunes – are melodies like 'The Sash', 'Derry's Walls' and 'The Billy Boys'. The first is an unmistakably catchy collection of chords, viewed with equal measure of affection and antipathy by the two communities. The 'Sash' is the most famous or infamous, depending on your point of view, of all Orange songs and the lyric of the first verse says it all:

> It is old but it is beautiful, and its colours they are fine,
> It was worn at Derry, Aughrim, Enniskillen and the Boyne.
> My father wore it when a youth in the by-gone days of yore,
> So on the Twelfth I always wear the sash my father wore.

'The Billy Boys' is a real 'belter' of a tune, containing the additional lyric, 'We're up to our necks in Fenian blood … surrender or you'll die'. Such is the gusto with which it is sung that sometimes the opening few bars have been sufficient to spark trouble. The fact that these songs have frequently been played loudest by some bands while passing nationalist areas and Catholic churches has done little to promote the notion of the Twelfth as a festival for all.

According to Neil Jarman, parading has been an integral part of the sectarian conflict north of the border. He points out that the Troubles began with disputes over protest marches by the Civil Rights Movement and the opposition parades organised by the Democratic Unionist Party and others. He talks about 'an inevitable symmetry' when the nationalist community objected to the Orange and Apprentice Boys parades. In his view,

> The descent into conflict was pushed by parades and then, as we eased out of it, the parades once again came

to the fore as we shifted away from the use of the gun and the bomb, towards a more social and political contest. The parades were part of that move back onto the democratic platform with challenges to the right to demonstrate and freedom of expression issues.

He also points out that throughout the years of the Troubles, the Orange Order voluntarily rerouted many of its parades.

Divisions and tensions arising from contentious parades have impacted negatively upon large sections of the community. For two centuries, in well-documented incident after well-documented incident, murder and serious injury have been the constant companions of parade-linked violence. In the final decade of the twentieth century, with the advent of satellite communication and twenty-four-hour rolling news programmes, the 'parades problem' was brought to the attention of a worldwide audience and it was encapsulated in one word — Drumcree.

CHAPTER 4

DRUMCREE

The British Army sent its top soldier, Sir Mike Jackson, to Drumcree in 1996. The BBC sent its top correspondent Kate Adie. The Orangemen protesting on the hill in front of the church erected a large placard, which read: 'It must be war, Kate Adie's here!'

It was not war, but this annual confrontation – centred on a picturesque parish church perched on top of a drumlin in County Armagh just north of Portadown – impacted upon the entire population of Northern Ireland. The 150-year-old Church of the Ascension seems an unlikely place for such a conflict, although it does have a lineage connecting it with past military campaigns. Inside the porch hangs an old union flag, which was used by pall-bearers to drape over the dead of the first World War. It was brought back to Drumcree by the rector at that time, who'd experienced the carnage in France as an army chaplain. The flags of church youth organisations sit alongside a British Legion standard, further emphasising the historic link with the crown forces. The architecture is unusual for a small country parish, with sweeping hand-carved arches buttressing sturdy pillars. Every Sunday the thick stone walls resound to a familiar form of Anglican worship that is representative of the most conservative brand of unionism in this particular corner of Northern Ireland. During the height of the violence associated with the Drumcree protests, the inside of this church was the calm in the eye of the storm.

ORGANISED INTIMIDATION

There are many origins to this dispute, which frequently overshadowed a shaky fledgling peace process. For some those origins lay in the years of suppression of a sizeable Catholic minority on the outskirts of proudly loyalist Portadown. For others it was in Obins Street in the 1980s when the RUC, for the first time, baton-charged Orangemen intent on parading their traditional route through a Catholic enclave. For others it came about through perceived double-dealing and a triumphalist hand-in-hand walk by two politicians who would vie for the leadership of unionism in the North. For the Portadown Orangemen it all began one Sunday afternoon at the end of their annual July church service and the dispute was to become one of the ugliest manifestations of conflicting rights ever encountered since the formation of the Northern Ireland state.

Support for the Drumcree dispute took many guises, but one of its more sinister and intimidatory faces involved hundreds of Orangemen and loyalist paramilitaries organising barricades and manning road blocks on the major arterial road networks across Northern Ireland. The co-ordinated street protests impacted on Catholics and Protestants simultaneously to an extent that had not been seen since the 1970s.

The RUC was accused of standing back and allowing roads to be blocked and to remain impassable. In early July each year the International Airport near Belfast took on the appearance of a mass evacuation centre, as thousands flocked to the check-in desks in an unseemly rush to exit the country before Drumcree got underway. On one occasion the airport itself was blockaded by Drumcree supporters and the roads for miles around were jammed with the cars as frustrated families of holiday-makers lugged their heavy cases by foot to the airport terminal. The port of Larne in County Antrim, Northern Ireland's main ferry terminal, was also paralysed. One of those present at the blockade on the main road to the port was the area's unionist MP. He told reporters that he was only there observing that it all passed off peacefully.

Belfast was badly affected. Employers, fearing the worst, sent their staff home early around Drumcree time. Stores, offices, shops, restaurants, cinemas and pubs all closed at lunchtime, turning the city into a ghost town by mid-afternoon. At the height of summer with the sun beating down on the empty streets, the city centre resembled a post-apocalyptic film set. All that was missing was some tumbleweed blowing along the deserted footpaths and carriageways.

As dusk fell, palls of smoke could be seen rising into the air from the burning barricades erected in loyalist areas around the city. Fear ruled and everywhere the tension was unmistakeable. The Drumcree protests became a watershed moment for the Orange Order, the Church of Ireland, the police and the main unionist political parties and it took Northern Ireland right to the edge.

THE RIGHT TO MARCH

To fully understand how this set of extraordinary circumstances came about it is necessary to put Drumcree, and the issue of contentious parades generally, into some sort of historical context.

The vast majority of Orange marches are not contentious. The problems arise in areas where a republican or nationalist community objects to a parade passing through or close to their area. In the mid-nineties, Garvaghy Road became the contentious 'cause célèbre' of the nationalist community in Northern Ireland. Neil Jarman says,

> The Orange Order's claim of an absolute right to march along the Queen's highway was something that was never extended to the nationalist community. The origins of the Drumcree dispute go back to the mid-1980s when a group of nationalists who wanted to hold a St Patrick's Day parade in Portadown were prevented from doing so by unionists in the town. The following year there was a contrasting protest against one of the Orange parades. Since then there's been a continuing cycle of protests in Portadown and you could speculate that if that St Patrick's Day parade had gone ahead we might not be in the same situation over Drumcree.

Jarman says the Orange Order tore itself apart internally over Drumcree because it couldn't see the bigger picture. 'It could not see beyond getting down the Garvaghy Road.'

DRUMCREE BEGINS

Drumcree means 'ridge of the branch or leafy tree' and it's believed it was once a centre for Druidism in Ireland. Christianity has been practised here since Celtic times with the Culdees of Armagh taking control in the sixth century. They were an ancient monastic order who some Presbyterian historians credit with keeping primitive Christianity 'free from the influence of Rome' in this part of northern Europe.

More recently it has been a place of worship for people of the Church of Ireland. In 1807 the Portadown District Lodge began attending services at Drumcree church – claimed by them to be the oldest Orange church parade in the world – to give thanks to God for the victory of William, Prince of Orange in upholding the reformed Protestant faith.

Twelve years earlier and just a few miles away, a number of parishioners from Drumcree had been involved in the Battle of the Diamond. One of the first clergymen to join the newly formed Orange Order was the Reverend George Maunsil, who was the rector of Drumcree at that time.

When the Orangemen attended their inaugural service in the church in 1807 the sermon was preached by the Reverend Stewart Blacker, an Orangeman and father of Lt-Colonel William Blacker one of the early leaders of the Institution.

Portadown in County Armagh is known as the citadel of Orangeism and Drumcree parish is regarded as the 'mother church' of the bustling market town. It is steeped in Orange and Protestant folklore. These are stories from the Irish rebellion of the mid-seventeenth century when eighty Protestant men, women and children were forced off a bridge into a river by Catholics, where they drowned or were shot as they tried to escape.

In the late 1800s there were riots in the town over a Catholic parade, a Salvation Army band procession and an Orange march. The annual Drumcree Orange parade was a comparatively trouble-free affair until the onset of the Troubles in Northern Ireland, when spiralling sectarian conflict along with demographic changes in the suburbs of Portadown were combining to make a volatile political cocktail.

TUNNEL VISION

Breandan MacCionnaith led the Garvaghy Road Residents' Coalition throughout the worst years of the Drumcree protests. He had served a jail term for his part in a republican bomb attack in Portadown. He says the only time the Drumcree parade was entirely trouble free was during the 1940s because of the Second World War. Nationalist residents had been lobbying to have the Orange parade rerouted prior to the 1995 church service, but MacCionnaith says they were still surprised when it was stopped by the police that year. He says:

Of course you need to go back ten years to Obins Street in 1985 when the government banned the Orange from marching through there. Logically if the parade was being banned from going through the smaller of the Catholic areas in Portadown then it must follow that the Orangemen should be banned from marching down the larger nationalist area of the Garvaghy Road.

The SDLP, Sinn Féin and the local residents were lobbying for that throughout the eighties, but it didn't materialise. The Drumcree Faith and Justice Group – the forerunner of the Garvaghy Road Residents' Coalition – was formed and, along with the SDLP and Sinn Féin, lobbied to have Orange parades rerouted from the area. Breandan MacCionnaith says people remember an incident in the early seventies when 'the UDA had become involved with an Orange parade and men in paramilitary uniform had also marched down the Garvaghy Road.'

During that time Northern Ireland convulsed into widespread civil unrest. Portadown was home to some particularly active loyalist groups and also a target for IRA attacks. The newly-formed Ulster Defence Association – the largest loyalist paramilitary group – erected barricades in Protestant estates. Republicans too erected barriers in the nationalist Obins Street area. Even with the onset of the peace process twenty years later, the psychological barricades never really came down in Portadown.

In July 1972 the physical barriers erected in Obins Street, blocked the route of a planned Orange parade and the security forces were sent in to remove them. This sparked a riot involving republicans, but eventually the Orange march did go ahead. The parade was preceded by a group of about fifty UDA men dressed in paramilitary uniform, many of them masked or wearing dark glasses, who formed up on either side of the road leading to the Tunnel giving the impression of the UDA providing safe passage for the Orangemen. At this time the UDA was not a proscribed organisation and it portrayed itself as the 'defender of the Protestant people from the IRA'. It is not clear if the paramilitaries were there at the request of the Orangemen or if they recognised a propaganda opportunity and seized it unilaterally.

Whatever the reason, it was the equivalent of waving a red, white and blue flag at a republican bull. The IRA responded by threatening to stop future Twelfth parades along Obins Street.

The Catholic enclave near the centre of Portadown is on the 'other side of the tracks' and is linked to the rest of the town by a pedestrian tunnel under the main Belfast to Dublin railway line. Obins Street was part of the outward leg of the Drumcree church parade and members of the Royal Black Institution also paraded along this route before leaving for the annual Sham Fight in Scarva on 13 July. The Tunnel area was to become the first major obstacle to be faced by the Loyal Orders in Portadown.

By 1985 tit-for-tat tactics had been adopted by both sides. On St Patrick's Day that year a nationalist accordion band attempted to parade from Obins Street to the mainly nationalist Garvaghy Road, but it found the route blocked by police where it passed by a number of Protestant homes. Nationalists contrasted this with the way the police allowed Orange marches to go past their houses in Obins Street.

'There was never a formal nationalist parade through Portadown town centre,' says Breandan MacCionnaith,

That was one of the sparks which ignited Obins Street in 1985. The St Patrick's accordion band had been given permission to walk a circuit that would have included Obins

Street, Garvaghy Road and back down through Park Road. When the nationalist parade got underway it was stopped at the mainly loyalist Park Road. That contradiction, of Orangemen being able to march where they wanted in Portadown assisted by the security forces and then a nationalist band on St Patrick's morning being blocked while marching along a route that was mostly nationalist, was clear for everyone to see. It added momentum to the protests at that time because it was right in your face – there was one law for Orangemen and another law for nationalists in Portadown.

This led to a sit-down protest by nationalists on the morning of 7 July that year when the next Orange march was due through the Tunnel area. The police were forced to cordon off the Tunnel and the Orangemen did not get through. They were stopped again on the Twelfth morning and that was when the Orange balloon burst. There were violent clashes between the Orange marchers and the security forces. Television news crews were there to capture dramatic pictures of men wearing their best Sunday suits, bowler hats, Orange collarettes and white gloves attacking members of the Royal Ulster Constabulary with rolled-up umbrellas. These images were flashed across television screens in Northern Ireland and were deeply unsettling for many viewers. If there was shock amongst nationalists watching, it was nothing compared to what was being felt in certain sections of the Protestant community.

The spectacle of Orangemen, who swear allegiance to the crown and her Majesty's forces, in open and violent conflict with the Royal Ulster Constabulary seemed contradictory to all the Loyal Order and Protestantism stood for. It was a sight television viewers would get used to. Ten years later the first Drumcree stand-off took place and set in train a sequence of events that would paralyse large parts of Northern Ireland and bring the security situation to crisis point.

The continued objections of nationalists in Obins Street to Orange parades and the trouble surrounding them led to all further Orange marches being rerouted along the mainly loyalist Corcrain Road. This affected the outward route of the annual Drumcree church parade, but a much more serious development was pending which caught many people by surprise.

STOPPED AT DRUMCREE

On a Sunday afternoon before the Twelfth of July in 1995 the Portadown District Orangemen filed out of their annual Somme Remembrance service at Drumcree church on the outskirts of Portadown to find their homeward route blocked by the Royal Ulster Constabulary. Nationalist residents had staged a sit-down protest on the Garvaghy Road objecting to the parade going through their area on its return to Portadown. Breandan MacCionnaith explains:

> What you had every year as a result of the Orange parades was saturation of the area by the Brits and the peelers and a then a riot either the night before, the day of the parade or the day after it. So in 1995 we were looking to see how we could change that so that we didn't end up with a riot every year. We wanted to focus our people's energy into a

more constructive opposition. We started organising within the community and we met with the police advocating that the march be rerouted. We also sought meetings with the government, but pre-1995 they didn't appear particularly concerned.

Few could have realised at the time that this first stand-off would develop from a localised dispute into an event which would dominate the Northern Ireland security and political agenda for the next decade.

The demographic profile of the return route to Portadown from Drumcree church had changed drastically. A hundred years earlier when the lodges paraded back from the Drumcree Sunday service to the centre of Portadown, the now contentious Garvaghy Road was little more than a country lane. In the late sixties and early seventies the Ballyoran, Garvaghy Park and Churchhill Park housing estates were constructed along the route and a population of more than six thousand people moved in. The new communities were mixed to begin with, but gradually the Protestants moved out and more Catholics moved in and the area became predominantly nationalist. It is claimed that Protestants who were intimidated out of their homes were replaced by Catholics who had been intimidated out of theirs in other areas.

The Church of Ireland Primate at the time of the Drumcree dispute was Archbishop Robin Eames:

Drumcree church for 365 days of the year was a normal country parish church. The Orangemen had gone there for generations, parading on the Battle of the Somme anniversary. Nobody had ever said a word about it. Like hundreds of other services across Northern Ireland it passed off peacefully and there was no problem. Suddenly I was confronted with real trouble on the road from the church.

The nationalists had decided to test the waters by staging their own march down the Garvaghy Road into the town centre at the same time as the Orange parade was due to take place. The residents were stopped by RUC before reaching the town centre and the protestors had walked back up the Garvaghy Road and stood around the junction with Ashgrove Road. The police were unable to allow the Orange march to proceed because of the threat of public disorder if the two sides came into close proximity.

Breandan MacCionnaith blames the RUC for inciting the crowd onto the Garvaghy Road:

> We were not blocking the road at this time, however one of the senior police officers told us that we were and a warning was relayed over a loud hailer telling us that we were involved in an illegal protest and obstructing traffic. So we thought that since we were being accused of breaking the law then we might as well do it. So we moved onto the road and after about three hours a senior RUC officer came over and told us that the Orange parade was being rerouted.

That evening the Orangemen at Drumcree starting calling for support from all over Northern Ireland, people started arriving on the hill in large numbers.

The District Master of Portadown was Harold Gracey, who was to become the embodiment of unbending Orangeism. The police decision to reroute the parade had left him visibly shaken as he addressed his fellow Orangemen at Drumcree that Sunday. 'The brethren of Portadown will not be moving, let it be hours, let it be days, let it be weeks. We are for staying until such time as we can walk our traditional route down the Garvaghy Road.'

The DUP leader Ian Paisley and the local Ulster Unionist MP and future party leader David Trimble were among the politicians who turned up at Drumcree that year. David Trimble says, 'The particular events in 1995 did come as a bolt out of the blue. There was some concern being expressed amongst the District officers in Portadown before the parade that a fast one might be pulled on them.'

Indeed some senior Orangemen in Portadown had received an indication a few days earlier that the parade would be stopped. The singing of the British National Anthem at the end of the church service that Sunday was the signal for the police to close the road at Drumcree. The rector, the Rev John Pickering, recalls the scene outside his church that morning as the Orangemen lined up on the road with their parade route blocked by police.

'It was going to come to a head somewhere' he says, 'but the protest shouldn't have happened outside a church after Sunday service.'

The clergyman remembers saying to his late wife that day that they'd better get back to the rectory and have their dinner first, as it may take some time to resolve. 'Little did we know the protest would continue to the extent that it has, consuming half of my entire ministry as rector of Drumcree.'

Lord Trimble recalls that he and the local Orangemen had great difficulty trying to negotiate with RUC commanders during the first year of the protest.

'At the start, these officers simply wouldn't talk. They would meet us and just say "This is it, go home". It was really Ronnie Flanagan's intervention at the last minute that resolved the matter.'

Assistant Chief Constable Ronnie Flanagan was heavily involved in the mediation process that got underway as violence erupted at the police lines at Drumcree and elsewhere in Northern Ireland. The Lower Ormeau Road in Belfast was a growing concern to security chiefs as nationalist residents there objected to an Orange parade passing through their area on its way to Belfast city centre. The tension on the Ormeau was heightened by the Orange threat of diverting the entire Belfast Twelfth parade to the Ormeau area in support of the local Ballynafeigh lodges. With Drumcree and other protests elsewhere in the province to contend with, the prospect of thousands of Orangemen, bandsmen and their supporters descending on the Ormeau Road would have stretched the security forces to breaking point.

At Drumcree, meanwhile, the Portadown Orangemen refused to engage face-to-face with what they saw as a Sinn Féin-inspired residents' group. However, negotiations involving their political representatives, the RUC, the residents' group and the Mediation Network eventually led to a 'deal' being done. On the morning of 11 July, forty-six hours behind schedule, the Portadown District Orange Lodge paraded in silence down the Garvaghy Road. Nationalists who'd staged a sit-down protest, allowed themselves to be lifted off the road by police and they stood by the roadside with their backs turned as the Orangemen marched past. The precise nature of the deal that facilitated this is hotly disputed by both sides to the present day.

Breandan MacCionnaith outlines his version of events,

> An agreement was reached which we believed would mean a parade would go down the Garvaghy Road that day, on the condition that all future parades would be with the consent of the people living in the area. That was given to me by Ronnie Flanagan of the RUC in the presence of the Mediation Network on the Garvaghy Road. The march went ahead with only a handful of police on the road. Without an agreement there would have been two thousand cops on the road to get it down. Our people stood aside as the Orangemen marched by. Then as soon as the parade reached the bottom of the Garvaghy Road you had David Trimble stating that there had been no agreement and that the Orangemen had come down with their flags flying as they intended to do in the future. The District Master Harold Gracey also denied that there had been any agreement reached with the nationalist residents.

From a nationalist perspective, worse was to come. When the Orangemen reached Carleton Street Orange hall, David Trimble and Ian Paisley linked hands and with arms held aloft they paraded 'triumphantly' through the tumultuous crowd of cheering Orangemen. Breandan MacCionnaith and his supporters on the Garvaghy Road watched the television news pictures in dismay.

'It was a red flag to a bull,' says MacCionnaith. 'But at the same time we thought they may have been showboating and at the end of the day what we had to do over the next twelve months was to ensure that the agreement which we and the Mediation Network believed had been reached, was abided by. We were told that people from the Orange side were aware of the agreement and that it was deliverable.'

David Trimble denies that what became known as his 'victory jig' with Ian Paisley was done with the intention of goading the nationalist community in Portadown.

No, that was not planned in any way. The parade reached Carleton Street, the National Anthem was played and then the Orangemen turned and faced each other on either side of the road. Spontaneous applause broke out for the District Master Harold Gracey and he was encouraged to walk down between the ranks. Then someone called for me and someone called for Paisley. As I started to move I saw Paisley coming forward behind me. Now this was my constituency, I was the Member of Parliament for the area, he was not. I wasn't having that man walking down Carleton Street ahead of me and I could see that was about to happen. So I grabbed his hand to keep him back so that he wouldn't get past me and he couldn't refuse to take it. The TV cameras were there and it was portrayed in a certain way and of course the 'jig' never happened. That jig was as a result of some bloody television man re-cutting and speeding up the footage and I thought it was wholly improper.

Nevertheless, the sight and sound of Trimble and Paisley walking through the cheering ranks of Portadown District Orange Lodge was portrayed as triumphalist and it may have scuppered any hope of sorting out the Drumcree problem for years to come.

'I have got an awful lot of stick over it,' concedes David Trimble, 'and I won't quarrel with that observation. I think it was quite possibly how it was seen at the time. Certainly the way it was portrayed in the media and particularly the way that idiot in television turned it into a jig, I think some people think it actually was a jig. It certainly had a negative effect.'

The Garvaghy Road Residents' Coalition believed they'd been misled by the Assistant Chief Constable Ronnie Flanagan over an assurance which they say was given by him that there would be no future Orange parades down the Garvaghy Road without the residents consent. The seeds of discontent had effectively been sown for another stand-off the following year.

DRUMCREE 1996

By the time 'Drumcree Two' came round in 1996, Orange anger at the way they were being treated had crystallised into a splinter group within the Order calling itself 'The Spirit of Drumcree'. Its founding member was a militant Orangeman from County Tyrone. Joel Patton, who ran a market-gardening business, had been one of the first to answer the call to Drumcree the previous year to show his support for the stand that was being taken. As he mingled with the other Orangemen who had also answered the call for support at Drumcree, he found himself amongst several like-minded brethren who felt there was a failure in the Orange leadership. These Orangemen wanted to do more to stamp their authority on the parades issue. Within a few months the Spirit of Drumcree group had been formed and a rally had been organised for the Ulster Hall in Belfast. In the packed auditorium, scene of so many unionist rallies and famous loyal orations, one of the platform speakers had the large and enthusiastic crowd of 'spirited' Orangemen shouting and stamping their feet in support when he remarked that,

> Sectarian means you belong to a particular sect or organisation. I belong to the Orange Institution. Bigot means you look after the people you belong to. That's what I'm doing. I'm a sectarian bigot and proud of it.

There were thinly veiled threats from the platform about 'taking on the security forces if necessary' and there was talk of the brethren having to 'physically defend themselves'.

'But remember,' said the speaker, 'It's how this Order was founded ... in violence to defend the Protestant people.'

The Spirit of Drumcree followers were the shock troops of

the support campaign across Northern Ireland. Many SOD members thought it strange, however, that the Portadown District officers, while welcoming the support, seemed to want to have minimal close contact with them.

The newly installed County Grand Master of Armagh at the time was Denis Watson. He'd been proposed for the County position by Portadown's District Master, Harold Gracey. Watson gave him an undertaking that he would support the Portadown lodges in getting a resolution to the Drumcree problem. He was aware however that in his first year as County Master there was little likelihood of a quick fix,

> I remember taking all our bits and pieces with us in the car – sleeping bag, tent, laptop, fax machine anything that would be needed was all taken out to the hill at Drumcree. I remember my daughter saying to me that she couldn't understand why we were doing this. At school she was being told by others about all the 'awful things the Orangemen were doing to the poor people on the Garvaghy Road'. I told her that one day she'd realise why we were doing it.

Thousands of Orangemen flocked to Drumcree in 1996 to show their support for the Portadown lodges. A massive security operation was put in place to prevent the parade or its supporters from advancing towards the Garvaghy Road. Hundreds of soldiers and police were flown into the fields around Drumcree church by Chinook helicopters, which kicked up huge clouds of dust and dry grass upon landing, evoking scenes reminiscent of a foreign war zone.

The army erected a tented camp, including a field hospital, in the surrounding farm land. The world's media erected their own encampment of tented camera positions, satellite trucks and editing vehicles on the grass verges of the narrow road leading from Drumcree to the Garvaghy Road. The Chief Constable announced that the parade was being rerouted and everyone settled down for another violent stand-off. That Sunday night the loyalist and Orange protestors lived up to the security forces expectations with several thousand people subjecting the police and army to a hail of missiles, petrol bombs and exploding fireworks.

The following morning the news broke that a Catholic taxi driver from nearby Lurgan had been found shot dead in his vehicle. Michael McGoldrick, aged thirty-one, had graduated as a mature student from Queen's University a few days earlier. A maverick unit within the UVF in Portadown, which had breached the two-year-long Loyalist ceasefire, was blamed for the shooting. During the trial of the man convicted of the murder, it was revealed that Mr McGoldrick, a father of two, was killed by the breakaway UVF faction, which would later become the LVF, after plans to kidnap three Catholic priests from a parochial house in County Armagh were aborted. The priests were to be shot if the Orangemen were not allowed to walk down the Garvaghy Road.

The book *Lost Lives*, which chronicles all those killed during the Northern Ireland Troubles, includes Michael McGoldrick's father's appeal to loyalists and republicans after the funeral:

As I bury my son, both of you bury your pride. I don't want any mother or father going through what my wife and I went through today ... please stop this.

Few, if any were listening. The protests continued at Drumcree and elsewhere in Northern Ireland, with Catholic families forced to leave their homes because of attacks by loyalists. RUC resources were being stretched to the absolute limit and some police officers' homes and families were being attacked by Drumcree supporters. A popular slogan daubed on walls in Protestant areas at this time was 'Join the RUC and come home to a real fire.' According to police welfare officers, morale within the RUC was at breaking point. Some policemen had to be taken out of the line when they recognised relatives in the Orange ranks as they peered through the protective Perspex of their riot shields. Other officers were recognised by some of the protestors and endured vile chants about their wives and families back at home.

The violence from the Orange side of the barrier at Drumcree was relentless and also showed signs of being well co-ordinated. Protestant families, including young children, arrived at Drumcree each evening to express peaceful and lawful support for the Portadown Orangemen, but others arrived with ulterior motives.

Denis Watson recalls one occasion when he was with David Trimble at Drumcree:

We were walking down the hill along with Harold Gracey when suddenly David went ballistic after seeing this mechanical digger with metal plating welded onto it. Two men were still working at the diggers' armour plating so David climbed up and told them to stop what they were doing. But he was pushed off the vehicle and but for Harold Gracey's intervention I'm convinced he would have been killed. I remember David looking at me and saying that this armour plated digger was 'just not on'. I then turned to him and said that if he thought that was bad, they were intending to bring slurry spreaders filled with petrol to Drumcree. When he asked me what they were for I told him to use his imagination. I just remember his face going bright red.

David Trimble along with other political leaders was involved in ongoing negotiations with police commanders to try to defuse the increasingly explosive situation. The Church leaders, meanwhile, were brokering a talks process involving the Garvaghy Road residents and the Orangemen. These talks were arranged to take place in the Carpet Mills factory at the bottom of the Garvaghy Road.

The Church of Ireland Primate Robin Eames says in the circumstances they had to do something,

'I wouldn't have said it was a runner, but I would say it was the only chance of a runner because there was no other show in town.'

David Trimble had drawn up a plan linking the July Drumcree parade to improving community relations within Portadown. Nationalist residents continually complained they couldn't even go into the town to do their shopping.

Archbishop Eames says this was one of the first attempts to take a long term view of the situation while not allowing Drumcree to become totally isolated from the existing tensions elsewhere in Portadown,

It seemed to me that one of the good arguments in trying to convince the Garvaghy Road residents to go along with the deal, was that this might be longer-lasting than just the parade itself.

Breandan MacCionnaith of the Residents' Coalition says the Carpet Mills talks were going nowhere,

Eames produced a document at one stage along the lines that a St Patrick's Day parade could be held in Portadown town centre, but there would have to be an Orange march down the Garvaghy Road first.

Denis Watson remembers the document from Eames arriving via fax machine at Drumcree inviting the Portadown Orangemen into talks at a neutral venue.

Our meeting to discuss this document went on well into the night. Everybody put their tuppence worth in and it got hot and heavy at times, but in the end Portadown District Master Harold Gracey and his officers felt that if they were to go into these talks they would be compromised and it could cause all sorts of problems.

In the end Watson, along with his Deputy County Grand Master and County Grand Secretary, decided to attend because, 'we had nothing to lose and the worst thing that could happen to us was being run out of office.'

The Orangemen contacted Eames and indicated that they would attend the talks at the Carpet Mills as long as Breandan MacCionnaith of the Garvaghy Road Residents' Coalition was not in the same building. Even with this proviso the Portadown Orangemen were still jittery about the talks. Denis Watson recalls Harold Gracey contacting him the following morning after the decision had been taken to go to the Carpet Mills meeting,

> It was quite early as we prepared to leave Drumcree Hill and travel the short distance to the Carpet Mills. Harold came up to me and indicated that having spoken to some people overnight he wasn't happy about it and said we were not to go. I basically told him that it had already been agreed at the meeting the night before and I made it clear that I'd given my word to Archbishop Eames and I would not be reneging on that.

Watson recalls the rest of the Orange leaders had a novel way of dealing with the District Master,

> Harold was subsequently taken to the "senior officers only" room in the church hall, put under lock and key and kept there for the duration of the Carpet Mills talks.

Despite the Orangemen's stipulated precondition, Breandan MacCionnaith arrived with the Residents' Coalition delegation at the Carpet Mills factory that morning,

> We were met by Eames and Cardinal Cahal Daly, the Catholic Primate of Ireland and we were brought into a room and left there. Time went on and we asked one of the talks secretariat what was happening and could we speak to Archbishop Eames. He came back to us and said it was difficult because the Orange Order hadn't agreed to this. We said the discussions had been agreed the previous night around midnight and now we were being told there were obstacles. We felt that somebody hadn't been telling the truth the previous night when the talks were being set up.

Elsewhere in the building the County Lodge officers were also considering their options.

'I remember sitting in the room at the carpet mills looking through the glass panels,' says Denis Watson. 'We saw the Church leaders coming and going and then we spotted MacCionnaith in the building. We knew we were then on dicey ground because we'd already advised Eames that MacCionnaith being there would cause us a great problem. We realised the implications so we left immediately.'

The County officers were driven at speed back to Drumcree via the Garvaghy Road along the contested parade route. On the way, Watson took a call from Ronnie Flanagan requesting an urgent meeting. They agreed to see each other at the Drumcree rectory.

'When we arrived he asked me how quickly we could get the parade underway,' says Watson. 'I told him as quick as it would take me to walk across the fields to Drumcree church and tell the brethren.'

Denis Watson and the others crossed the field to Drumcree hill where he spoke to the Orangemen on the public address system, telling them to assemble in their lodges,

> The parade subsequently went down the Garvaghy Road into Portadown. I went with a few others to Carleton Street to meet the District Lodge arriving from Drumcree and I remember the Orangemen shaking our hands as they did so.

While Watson and his colleagues had left the Carpet Mills and returned to Drumcree, the residents' representatives still didn't know if the Orange delegation had even turned up for the talks, as Mr MacCionnaith explains:

> We heard there had been telephone conversations that morning between the Chief Constable and Eames. We phoned our people on the outside and told them that the talks were going nowhere and it was starting to look like a complete bluff. Then we heard that RUC vehicles were on the move and it looked like they were getting ready to take over the Garvaghy Road.

The residents say that two hours after arriving at the Carpet

Mills they asked to speak to Eames and were informed he was unavailable.

> We then heard that the police and army were moving onto the Garvaghy Road. I walked into the room where the church leaders were and I was quite angry. I told them that for Christian gentlemen they had brought us there on a complete con job and the talks were a farce.

Lord Eames denies conning the residents and maintains that he was as genuine about the Carpet Mills dialogue as they were.

> I think the residents' group representatives were willing to try. They were genuinely aghast when they heard the parade was going ahead. I remember MacCionnaith saying to me ... 'They're coming down the road and I have been betrayed'. He waved his mobile phone at us and led his delegation out of the factory and that was that. Any hope that plan had of breaking the ice went out the window at that stage.

Eames says he was never a party to any double dealing and he was not aware that the parade would eventually be forced down the road although he concedes the pressure on the security forces to defuse the situation was intense. The security forces' solution to 'bursting the bubble' on Drumcree hill was to put them down the Garvaghy Road.

Archbishop Eames believes that while the overriding

security considerations meant that time was at a premium, he
did not think that time was that short,

> I felt that they could have given us longer. I asked myself
> over the years since, 'Was the situation for the police and
> army really as serious as it was portrayed?' I repeatedly
> told the Secretary of State, Sir Patrick Mayhew, that he had
> to give us more time because we couldn't give him a solu-
> tion in a short period of time. He knew the talks were
> taking place and I would say he was willing to let it be
> tried and I think he was as frustrated as any of us in the
> end.

Denis Watson believes the security forces panicked when they
took the decision to force the parade down the road that day,

> We were getting close to the Twelfth and people were
> going to be totally stressed out. I think the police were
> afraid of more problems arising in other parts of the prov-
> ince and they were concerned that they wouldn't be able
> to cope with that.

Back on the Garvaghy Road, police in riot gear moved in to
clear away people who were sitting on the carriageway and the
atmosphere was highly charged. Witnesses say the Catholic Primate Cardinal Daly got a rough ride from angry residents when
he arrived back from the aborted Carpet Mills talks. At that time
it was thought that he had been an accessory to what they saw
as a bluff. It later transpired that he did not agree to a march

down the Garvaghy Road.

Archbishop Eames recalls the feelings among the clergy at that moment when the parade was put down the road,

> Cardinal Daly was feeling very betrayed. He'd already had a meeting on the Garvaghy Road with the residents and had taken some abuse. MacCionnaith told him that he'd been betrayed by coming into the talks process under the guise that they might reach some sort of agreement and then suddenly to be told even as we were meeting, that the parade was going ahead.

MacCionnaith claimed that the churchmen must have known what was going to happen all along, but this was strenuously denied by the clergy. Lord Eames remembers the ferocity he felt as they drove through the crowds at the bottom of the Garvaghy Road,

> The four Church leaders went to Seagoe rectory in Portadown for a cup of tea and to listen to developments on the radio news and to talk things over. Cahal Daly was the first to leave. It was obvious to me at that moment that he was deeply hurt and that he felt betrayed by the government. He'd understood that the parade would not be forced down the Garvaghy Road while there was any hope of getting a resolution of the problem.

The talks ended in a shambles and acrimony. In a sense they were over before they'd begun.

PLOTS AND CONSPIRACIES

Conspiracy theories were rife during the run-up to Drumcree '96. Suspicions were high that there were 'moles' within the ranks of the Orangemen who were feeding information back to the government, MI 5 and the security forces about the intentions of the Portadown lodges.

Denis Watson says he was tipped-off that his phones were being tapped and he explains that the County Orangemen went to great lengths to counter this,

> We adopted a cell structure similar to that of the IRA. Those people who needed to know knew. And those people who didn't need to know didn't know. We threatened the membership of County Armagh with very strong disciplinary measures if anybody stepped out of line or broke ranks regarding confidentiality. It worked very, very well.

Such was the level of control being exerted over matters of confidentiality that even David Trimble, the Ulster Unionist leader, was having trouble getting his nose through the door at times, 'We'd taken over a room at back of the Drumcree church hall and nobody was allowed into it except County and District lodge officers' explains Watson. 'At one stage Trimble's assistant came up and he was told he wasn't authorised to be there and he was put out of the room.'

When the Orange plan unfolded at Drumcree '96, parts of the country came to a standstill. On reflection, Denis Watson says it was horrific despite the fact that he was part of the team that helped to organise it:

> I remember ringing the Assistant Chief Constable Ronnie
> Flanagan one night at the height of the trouble and saying
> that we needed a meeting with him urgently. I'll never
> forget him saying down the telephone to me ... 'Where
> are you ... are you in the real world?' I said 'Yes, I'm out at
> Drumcree.' He then asked if I realised what was happen-
> ing across Northern Ireland. I replied that I'd seen some
> pictures on the television news. He responded by saying
> that the country was in a complete mess and uproar.

Watson concedes some of the protestors supporting the
Drumcree stand went too far. He says, 'the violence was despi-
cable and to see Belfast city centre deserted by mid-afternoon
... that was never our intention.'

A WORD IN THE WRIGHT EAR

Among the more sinister figures at Drumcree during this time
was the renegade UVF member Billy Wright, who was soon to
lead the LVF. He was a well-known figure around Portadown
and, because of his high profile in the media, throughout the
rest of Northern Ireland as well. For many hard-line loyalists he
was a paramilitary hero. To the Catholic community he was a
ruthless, merciless, sectarian killer.

When it emerged that the Ulster Unionist leader David Trimble
had had a face-to-face meeting with Wright at Drumcree in 1996,
the people living on the Garvaghy Road started asking themselves
what was really going on. David Trimble explains his reasoning

for engaging with the leading paramilitary at that time,

> I was trying to get agreement to this compromise. Basi-
> cally I wanted Wright on board because he had influence.
> Just as at the sharp end of the Garvaghy Road Residents'
> protest there were republicans who were prepared to sit
> down on the road to prevent the Orange parade passing,
> Wright and his people could do physically the same thing
> on the loyalist side. If they made it absolutely clear that
> they were going to stop any St Patrick's Day parade
> through Portadown, that would wreck the whole thing. I
> thought to myself I have got to make sure that this chap
> doesn't derail this.

As it turned out the Trimble proposal didn't get far because
the talks foundered.

While the police maintained overall command of the security situation on the ground, senior RUC officers discussed with
the army the possible options if the growing numbers of
Orangemen and supporters at Drumcree were to overrun their
lines. The army's plan was quite simple, militarily: if the rioters
got as far as the Catholic housing estates around the Garvaghy
Road then they would be shot. Politically, and every other way
probably, it was difficult to imagine a worse scenario. Breandan
MacCionnaith describes the situation:

> Despite the fact that we believed we'd reached an agree-
> ment in 1995, here were these Orangemen not happy with
> what happened the previous year, but going a step further

by bringing the entire six counties into it. Cardinal Daly saw any march along the Garvaghy Road, given what was happening in the North, not just as a humiliation for the Catholics in Portadown but a complete humiliation for the entire Catholic community across the North of Ireland.

MacCionnaith says that any initiative that emanated from the Orange or unionist side from 1996 onwards was always conditional on … 'march first, agreement after'.

In the immediate aftermath of the 1996 parade some senior figures within Orangeism were starting to consider alternatives for future years at Drumcree, even if they did appear to be as 'rare as hens' teeth'. A growing number of Orange Order members elsewhere in Northern Ireland watching the violence at Drumcree unfold year on year, were becoming increasingly concerned about what was being done in their name.

DRUMCREE 1997

The decision was taken to once again push the parade down the Garvaghy Road in 1997. As soldiers worked late into the night erecting barbed wire barriers across the fields and on the bridge below Drumcree church, few suspected that the police would use the cover of darkness to clear Garvaghy Road to make way for the parade to proceed the following day. About 3 am, with all but the most suspicious nationalist residents having retired to bed, two hundred Land Rovers trundled over the hill and down the Garvaghy Road. As some people attempted to sit in front of them on the road, a hand-operated Second World War air-raid siren roused the shocked residents from their sleep. There were sustained angry clashes between the crowd and police officers who were kitted out in new all-black riot gear. Makeshift barriers were set alight, petrol and acid bombs were lobbed and plastic bullets were fired during a rolling scrum of a riot that lasted two hours. Eventually the District Mobile Support Units cleared the road.

Ronnie Flanagan, who was by now the Chief Constable, explained his decision to impose the massive security operation upon the nationalist community, describing it as 'the balancing of two evils'. It was to be the last time Orange feet would walk on the Garvaghy Road.

The Residents' Coalition knew there were no guarantees that a parade would not be let down the road, despite a change in government at Westminster. The Coalition had met with a range of people that year including political parties and the Irish government. The County Armagh lodge officers had taken a more pro-active role in the 1997 dispute by launching their own charm offensive with opinion formers and people not normally seen as being well disposed towards Orangeism. They included the US government, President Clinton's office and the new Labour government. In June of that year Denis Watson, the County Grand Master, and the Rev. William Bingham, the County Grand Chaplain, wrote an open letter to the Garvaghy Road residents. It set out the tradition of the Drumcree parade and, while acknowledging the objections raised by nationalists, listed measures taken by the District Orange lodge to address some of them. These included placing restrictions on the number of parades each year and who would actually take part in them and introducing Orange marshals to make sure the march passed off peacefully and quickly.

The Secretary of State Mo Mowlam welcomed the letter as 'a sincere and genuine attempt to promote understanding'. The nationalist residents, meanwhile, were also hoping to woo the new power at Stormont.

Breandan MacCionnaith says,

> Mo Mowlam came down to meet us on the Garvaghy Road after Labour's victory in the general election. We were very conscious that the outgoing Tory government had been very dependent on Northern Ireland unionist politicians' votes to actually stay in power prior to that. With Labour's clear majority in parliament we were thinking that Trimble and company could not apply the same pressure on this government as they had during the previous Drumcree protest.

Despite this, the residents starting hearing whispers and read reports in the press about talks taking place that they weren't involved in.

MacCionnaith told the media he had no knowledge of any discussions and voiced his concerns about the reports,

> We'd been told by Mowlam that the decision on the parade would be relayed to us in time to mount a legal challenge in the High Court if necessary, but we had heard nothing. On the Saturday evening before the parade, I took a call from an angry Mo Mowlam. She told me that she was 'extremely pissed-off' over what I'd said about her

on the television news that evening. I responded that unless she was telephoning to tell me that she'd reached a decision on the parade, or to tell me what the talks were about that were apparently taking place without the residents, then I would continue saying what I'd said to the media.

The Orange parade was forced down the Garvaghy Road the following day and MacCionnaith says,

'I swore that I would never speak to that woman again and I never did speak to her again.'

The Orange side had kept up their contact with the Secretary of State and on the Saturday before the parade Denis Watson, who was about to go into a meeting with the Chief Constable at RUC headquarters, took a call from Ulster Unionist leader David Trimble who was about to meet Mo Mowlam,

He asked me what I wanted him to say to the Secretary of State. I told him to tell her that the parade had to go down the Garvaghy Road the following day or else he would pull all the Ulster Unionists out of the ongoing and finely balanced political talks process. His comment back to me was – 'you can't be serious'. I replied that I was very serious and that was the end of the conversation.

Watson says during his meeting at Police headquarters the Chief Constable tried to beat down the Orange on numbers. 'He asked us if we could come down the road with a hundred men or could we come down with this number of that number

... but I told him that either the full parade comes down the Garvaghy Road or nothing comes down it.'

That Saturday night at Drumcree Watson was called by a senior police officer on the ground in Portadown,

> He told me that we would probably see some movement on the security forces side of the cordon, but we shouldn't be alarmed because it was not what we would think it was. At this stage there was nothing to indicate that the parade would be going ahead the following morning.

By daybreak the early morning radio news bulletins were carrying the story about what had happened overnight on the Garvaghy Road. Some journalists who had also fallen for the ruse and hadn't heard the news bulletins turned up at Carleton Street and were initially surprised and bemused by the joyous demeanour of the Portadown Orangemen.

Denis Watson denies that the Orange Order was party to a secret deal with the police in 1997,

> We'd expressed our opinions about why the Orangemen should be allowed down the Garvaghy Road, but we were never told why the parade was put through that year. Technically it was a forced parade and we probably stupidly thought we'd solved the problem. Afterwards we all headed off on our holidays, feeling we didn't need to do any more work on the issue as we'd got the parade back in place and that's probably the mistake we made.

DRUMCREE 1998

The Public Processions (Northern Ireland) Act 1998 became law in February of that year, which led to the Drumcree march being banned from entering the Garvaghy Road not by the police, but by the newly formed Parades Commission. It was now the task of the forces of law and order to uphold that decision.

Violence ensued in loyalist areas as the standoff continued throughout the week leading up to the Twelfth of July demonstrations. There were threats of holding a mass Twelfth of July demonstration at Drumcree bringing tens of thousands of people onto the hill and face-to-face with the security forces. Community tensions throughout Northern Ireland were growing by the day as the countdown to the Twelfth ticked away like a time-bomb. People feared something terrible was going to happen.

On the morning of Sunday 12 July, a week into the 'Drumcree Four' stand-off, a very solemn Chief Constable was interviewed on BBC television and radio. Upon being greeted with a good morning by the interviewer, Ronnie Flanagan retorted that it was anything but a good morning for Northern Ireland. He then went on to grimly outline the overnight tragedy that had taken place in Ballymoney in County Antrim when three young brothers died in an arson attack on their home. He described their deaths as 'brutal sectarian murders'.

His words sent a shiver through the ranks of the Order and struck at the hearts of people in Northern Ireland and beyond. The previous week's news had been dominated by the violent protests arising out of the Drumcree standoff.

'What we've seen during the week is a hijacking of those

protests,' said Flanagan. 'What went on last night wasn't protest. We believe we're investigating the sectarian murder of three children – Richard, Mark and Jason Quinn asleep in their beds. That's not protest … that's murder.'

The most senior law enforcement officer in Northern Ireland was clearly laying the blame for the killings at the feet of the Drumcree protesters.

The murders of the three little boys aged ten, nine and eight, shocked everybody. The Democratic Unionist leader Dr Ian Paisley, in whose constituency they happened, was interviewed at the scene that rain-soaked morning. Standing in front of the blackened exterior of the house where the three children had died he told reporters:

> I understand this is a mixed marriage and I understand the three children went to a Protestant school. It had been said that they were Roman Catholics, but it doesn't matter what their religion was. This is a diabolical and evil deed.

In the wake of the murders, First Minister of the Stormont Assembly David Trimble and his Deputy Seamus Mallon both urged the Orangemen to end their protest at Drumcree.

The most telling response – which resonated most across Northern Ireland and particularly with many of his fellow Orangemen – came from one of the leading figures in the Drumcree dispute.

The Rev. William Bingham, a Presbyterian minister in Pomeroy in County Tyrone, was also the County Grand Chaplain of Armagh and had been part of the Drumcree Orange negotiating team for several years. Leaning heavily on the lectern in his church in Pomeroy that Sunday morning, with his Orange collarette draped around his clerical dog-collar, he spoke the words that many had been thinking but few were prepared to utter;

After last nights atrocious act, a fifteen-minute walk down the Garvaghy Road by the Orange Order would be a very hollow victory because it would be in the shadow of three coffins of little boys who wouldn't even know what the Orange Order is about.

As I stood at Drumcree this week, I asked myself this question – Brethren, where are we going? And where are we allowing ourselves to be led? The throwing of blast bombs at the RUC, is that Orangeism? If it is, I will have no part in it. The verbal attacks on people who think differently than we do. Is that Orangeism? If it is, I will have no part in it. The violence that we've seen, if that's Orangeism then many of us here will have no part in it. You and I know it's not Orangeism. You and I know that we have done our utmost and our best to make sure that all our protests are non-violent and peaceful ... but last night there was the evidence that things have got out of control, that we can no longer control the situation. And the great fear is that things will get worse and that more children's lives will be lost. Put yourself in the place of that family in Ballymoney. If that was your home, your children, your grandchildren, how would you feel today? How would you feel about the people who, out of principle did that?

No road is worth a life.

Ronnie Flanagan increased the pressure on the Grand Orange Lodge officers to use their influence to end the stand-off at Drumcree in the wake of the Quinn murders.

Denis Watson recalls how this led to a showdown between the hierarchy and Portadown District,

> All the County Grand Masters and Grand Lodge officers were summoned into Orange headquarters in Belfast for an urgent meeting. It was agreed that some people including the Grand Master Bobby Saulters, would travel to Portadown to talk to the Portadown Orangemen. Harold Gracey, the District Master, convened a meeting of the Portadown District Officers and the County and Grand Lodge officers at a loyal Order hall in the countryside, a few miles from Drumcree off the Dungannon Road.

The meeting was described as 'hot and heavy' with the Grand Master stating that the violence could not go on and the situation needed to be resolved. It was suggested that in the circumstances the honourable thing to do was accept the right of being able to walk along the Garvaghy Road but to refuse it and return to Portadown via the outward route thus bringing the protest to an end.

'The Portadown District Officers would have none of it,' says Watson who was at the meeting. 'The Grand Master, Bobby Saulters, and some of the County Grand Masters left that meeting with their tails between their legs … the Grand Lodge officers, including the Grand Master, were totally dismissed by the Portadown Orangemen.'

Despite the Quinn murders and the appeals for calm, the violence continued at Drumcree that Sunday night and for several nights afterwards. Rioters attacked the police and army with a renewed vigour and the security forces replied with dozens of plastic bullets being fired. Senior figures within Portadown District lodge were tiring of the wanton violence and a strategy was beginning to take shape to stop it happening again. Meanwhile the Bingham sermon had struck a heavy blow within the Order and as support drained away Drumcree four was effectively over.

The Portadown District Lodge condemned the murders, but refused to accept that the Drumcree protests had any bearing on them. The Grand Orange Lodge, however, in condemning the killings accepted that they were sectarian. By October of the following year, a court judgement stated that the Quinn murders were a combination of a sectarian attack by the UVF and a personal grudge against a relative of the children. The Rev. William Bingham called on the RUC to confirm there was no link between the murders and the Drumcree protest. He said the Chief Constable's remarks on the morning of the murders had weighed heavily on his mind when he used the term 'no road is worth a life'.

The Rev. Bingham said, 'I fully understand the deep sense of hurt experienced by the good and decent Orangemen of Portadown and Ballymoney and regret if in any way I added to their hurt at that time.'

To this day, many Orangemen believe the murders of the

Quinn children had nothing to do with Drumcree and they are convinced the Chief Constable used the tragedy to weaken support for Drumcree by discrediting the Orange Order. Flanagan has denied exploiting what happened in Ballymoney, maintaining that the murders were sectarian and followed a week of sectarian attacks and widespread intimidation. While he used the word 'protests' in his media interviews on the morning of the killings, he did not mention Drumcree specifically and is quoted more recently as stating, 'I think people judged for themselves whether they wanted to continue to support this protest.'

Loyalist areas of Portadown continued to flare up weeks after the parade was blocked, and in an incident linked to the Drumcree dispute in September, RUC officer Frankie O'Reilly was fatally wounded. The Catholic policeman was hit by a blast bomb on the loyalist Corcrain Road. Portadown District Orange Lodge Press Officer, David Jones, described the young policeman's death as 'a tragedy'. He added that the protest at Drumcree would continue saying:

'Unfortunately when you are standing up for liberties, sometimes the cost of those liberties can be very high.'

The Chairman of the Police Authority at the time, Pat Armstrong, described that statement as 'a deplorable insult to the memory of a brave police officer who gave his life in the service of the community.'

DRUMCREE 1999

The British government instigated a fresh round of talks involving the Orange Order and GRRC led by Prime Minister Tony

Blair's Chief of Staff at Downing Street, Jonathan Powell, in the latter half of 1998. The involvement of such a high-ranking civil servant was an indication of the seriousness with which the government was treating the looming 'Drumcree five'. The historic surroundings of the Palace Stables in Armagh, part of what was once the home of the Church of Ireland Primate, were set aside for the latest attempts at a negotiated settlement. Face-to-face meetings between Orangemen and Breandan MacCionnaith and the residents was still a non-starter as far as the loyal Order was concerned.

Breandan MacCionnaith explains,

> Jonathan Powell used two facilitators, Peter Quinn, (a Fermanagh businessman with a prominent background in the Gaelic Athletic Association) who worked with the residents and the Rev. Roy Magee (a Dundonald Presbyterian minister who'd been involved in brokering the loyalist paramilitary ceasefire) who worked with the Orange side. The gist of the talks was about finding some way of getting the Orangemen off the hill at Drumcree.

The discussions lasted from July 1998 to the end of the year and were accompanied, says MacCionnaith, 'by Drumcree-associated violence involving the intimidation of nationalists and the burning of Catholic property.'

In the early part of 1999, Frank Blair, the Director of the Advisory Conciliation and Arbitration Service (ACAS) was drafted-in to help break the impasse. His expertise in resolving disputes and building harmonious relationships in the workplace did not extend to Drumcree. His proposals were rejected by the Orangemen as an attempt to buy them off by offering one final parade down the Garvaghy Road in return for a multi-million pounds investment to regenerate in Portadown.

The gloom hanging over the proceedings grew even darker in March of that year when Rosemary Nelson, the GRRC legal advisor, was murdered by loyalists who placed a bomb under her car at her home in Lurgan.

When Drumcree Sunday came around amidst the usual welter of rising tensions, the Portadown Orangemen did a surprise 'about turn' at the security barrier. The lodges made their protest to the police commander then marched back up the hill to the church and dispersed. It later emerged that some of the senior figures, including District Master Harold Gracey, believed the government had promised them a parade down the Garvaghy Road later that year if they could keep a lid on things that Sunday. Tony Blair had a very different understanding of what was agreed and a parade that year wasn't part of it.

After most of the Orangemen had left the hill there were some clashes at police lines, but it was nothing like the violence of previous years. The rioting on the eleventh night at the nearby loyalist Corcrain estate, however, was prolonged and vicious. An effigy of a policeman in full riot gear was burnt on top of the bonfire. It was an obvious reference to Constable Frankie O'Reilly and mirrored the degree of antipathy between the loyalist protestors and the police. An RUC water cannon was used and plastic bullets were fired in response to petrol bombs and blast bombs thrown at the security forces and towards nearby Catholic homes.

DRUMCREE 2000

The Portadown Orangemen were back with a bang. After the peaceful 'about turn' the previous year, it now looked as if they were once more in belligerent mood as District Master Harold Gracey addressed the crowds gathered at the steel security barrier blocking their progress from Drumcree church,

> This battle is not just about Drumcree. This is about the Orange Order. It is about the Protestant people. They used to be on their knees, now they are on their bellies. If they don't get off their bellies before it's too late this country will be gone. I say to Tony Blair today, last year you may have duped us. You'll not dupe us this year.

This was also the year that Johnny 'Mad Dog' Adair, the notorious UFF leader from the lower Shankill in Belfast appeared on Drumcree hill. He arrived along with a group of his henchmen, dressed in white T-shirts emblazoned with the slogan 'UFF – Simply the Best.' For good measure Adair, who'd recently been released from prison under the terms of the Good Friday Agreement, brought his German shepherd dog 'Rebel' with him. The sight of this sort of loyalist muscle amidst the Orangemen milling about on Drumcree hill did little to dispel the fears of a further escalation of violence.

The calls went up once again for supporters of the stand being taken at Drumcree to come out onto the streets. The worst of the violence was again concentrated at the security barrier and the police and army lines at Drumcree. In Belfast shops, offices and businesses closed early. Even civil servants were sent home at lunchtime in case they got caught up in the night-time protests. The closures did not amount to support for the Orangemen; the business owners pulled down the shutters through fear of what would happen if they did not.

The Order seemed once again to be in disarray as its leaders issued contradictory statements while being accused of cowardice for refusing to publicly face down the loyalist paramilitaries who were wreaking violence in the name of Orangeism. It was the beginning of the end. As each year went by the enthusiasm for carrying on the protest at Drumcree seemed to reside solely within a hard core of Portadown Orangemen and even some of them were wavering. As the eleventh night bonfire embers died across Northern Ireland, so too did the heat generated by Drumcree. In subsequent years, the numbers of protesters dwindled amid a dawning realisation that, with Parades Commission criteria unmet and a changing political climate, there would be no return parade via the Garvaghy Road.

THE FALL-OUT

The violent protests associated with the Drumcree dispute impacted on communities across Northern Ireland. There was much sorrow, hurt and personal loss experienced by individuals and the victims' families. It can also be argued with justification that the protests did irrevocable damage to Orangeism, Protestantism, loyalism and Anglicanism.

Lord Eames, who was Church of Ireland Primate at the time,

was criticised from within and outside his Church for not calling a halt to the Drumcree church parades,

> The dilemma I faced was that this was a trustee Church ... all I could do was offer moral advice and leadership. I could ultimately have stopped the church service taking place by withdrawing the license of the rector to officiate at it. But to do that is a major, major step. I don't remember anybody doing that in my lifetime. You just don't do it simply for one occasion and then afterwards say, 'Well I'll give you your license back when it's all over." If you withdraw a rector's license that is virtually the end – he's out.

There was criticism also from bishops and clergy throughout the Church of Ireland over what was taking place at Drumcree, however, Lord Eames is adamant there was no alternative because to have denied the Orangemen access to the church would have meant the balloon going up,

> It wasn't easy explaining that to Church of Ireland people in Dublin. The further away from Drumcree you were the more difficult it was to understand what was going on. People in the Republic saw Drumcree church being used as some sort of cover for the UVF, the LVF and the UDA. Drumcree damaged the Church of Ireland from the point of view of the south. People in the Republic began to say that parishioners north of the border weren't really the same Church of Ireland as them, even though many parishioners at Drumcree found it impossible to take on

board what was happening outside their church in the early years of the protest. The genuine congregation at Drumcree will never forgive the Church of Ireland in the Republic for the criticism it poured on them.

To this day Drumcree parish withholds contributions to anything that could be interpreted as an all-Ireland church project. It's become part of the folklore that the congregation is not understood by the wider Church of Ireland, by its General Synod or by their co-religionists south of the border.

MacCionnaith says as far as nationalists on the Garvaghy Road are concerned, parades are no longer an issue.

The last Orange march along the Garvaghy Road was in 1997 and Portadown is now getting inward investment and it's starting to develop. There's been a tailing-off of sectarian incidents around the various interfaces in the town. There is an uneasy, but peaceful, equilibrium and only a madman would try to upset that. It might not be perfect, but it's got to the stage that all that violence, all that intimidation, all that tension has disappeared.

There is also an awareness that the easiest way of upsetting that delicate balance is by granting a parade against the wishes of the people of the Garvaghy Road.

Neil Jarman of the Institute for Conflict Research believes Drumcree, and the wider parading issue, has weakened Orangeism:

I think a large part of the fault lies with the Orange Order itself. Tactically they played it very, very badly. They started off by believing they were in the same position they were in during the late-nineteenth or early-twentieth century. At that time they could play the Orange card and everything would fall into place. They didn't recognise that this was a changed political dimension.

Jarman believes the state had a five-year strategy from 1995 to 2000 to break the power of Orangeism by challenging it, confronting it and finally putting it in its place,

Unfortunately from the Orange point of view, they walked right into a cul-de-sac without knowing how to get out of it or without a strategy to get beyond it. Drumcree 1996 took people within Northern Ireland and the Orange Order to a place they didn't want to go. That was one of the key elements in reshaping Orangeism. The middle ground of non-member supporters within the Protestant community were pushed further away and Orangemen who regarded themselves as being respectable and conservative just walked away from it and haven't come back.

Lord Eames cautions against complacency over the Drumcree issue,

I think now [in 2006] it is dangerous to hear people on the Garvaghy Road saying ... 'Forget about Drumcree ... it's over.' It's not over. There may be very few Orangemen going down to the police line after Sunday service to

Above: Hilda Winter outside 'Diamond' Dan Winter's cottage near Loughgall in County Armagh.

Below: United in Orangeism: Tommy and Leena Lynch from Drumaloor in County Cavan.

Above: Mohawk Loyal Orange Lodge 99 pictured in 1990 at their Orange hall near Toronto.

Below: The start of a long walk; Orangemen leave Clifton Street Orange hall in north Belfast as the city's main Twelfth of July Orange parade sets off.

Above: Orange Order Grand Master Robert Saulters greets the President of Ireland, Mary McAleese, in Áras an Uachtaráin in Dublin.

Below: Drew Nelson, Grand Secretary of the Orange Order.

Above: Soldiers man the barricades at the normally peaceful Drumcree church in preparation for the rerouted Orange Order parade.

Below: Portadown District Lodge marching down the Garvaghy Road between the lines o police landrovers. Directly behind and to the left of the bannerette is David Burrows (with moustache), Deputy District Master. Controversially, he later became a member of the Parades Commission.

Above: Breandan McCionnaith of the Garvaghy Road Residents' Coalition, with Martin McGuinness of Sinn Féin. MacCionnaith later became a Sinn Féin political advisor, but resigned from the party in March 2007 over its policy on accepting policing in Northern Ireland.

Below: Portadown District marches up to the security barrier at Drumcree church, the scene of violent confrontation for years between Orangemen and their supporters and the security forces.

Above: Orangemen argue at Pomeroy, County Tyrone on the Twelfth Day after Spirit of Drumcree men protested against Rev. William Bingham who called for an end to the Drumcree protest.

Below: The funeral of Richard, Mark and Jason Quinn.

Above: Gerry Kelly outside a Belfast courthouse in 1999 after claiming he was assaulted by police during a protest against an Orange Parade. The Sinn Féin MLA became a Junior Minister in the power sharing executive at Stormont in 2007.

Right: William of Orange mural in Coleraine, 1982.

Above: (L-R) David McConaghie of the Independent Orange Order, Robert Saulters, Grand Master of the Orange Order and William Logan, Sovereign Grand Master of the Royal Black Institution as they speak to the press following the meeting between the Loyal Orders and the SDLP.

Below: A historic moment – Paisley and Adams side-by-side, Stormont, 16 March 2007. (L-R) Nigel Dodds MP, DUP deputy leader Peter Robinson, DUP leader Rev. Ian Paisley, Sinn Féin President Gerry Adams, Sinn Féin Chairperson Mary Lou McDonald and Martin McGuinness MP at the Stormont Assembly building in Belfast.

make their protest, but that's not the point. There has not been a real solution to the Garvaghy Road issue. The Orangemen are maintaining that they've been rebuffed in attempts at dialogue by the Parades Commission, secondly by MacCionnaith and thirdly by the Northern Ireland Office and they feel very sore about that.

The former Primate views the Drumcree situation as a cameo of Northern Ireland with fear on both sides, the majority, the minority, violence and the manipulation of the situation by loyalist and republican paramilitaries. 'We can never, never, never assume that this is over until it is over.'

The Drumcree parade scenario continues to be played out annually and there is still no sense of a compromise being reached. In recent years, however, the massive security operations that surrounded the event have been dramatically scaled down to a few land rovers and a handful of police officers. The numbers of people turning out to support the stand taken by Portadown District has also been in decline and the violence that accompanied it has virtually disappeared.

The most startling development has been the appointment to the Parades Commission of David Burrows. The former Portadown Orangeman was Harold Gracey's deputy and then successor as District Master. He is a high profile Drumcree veteran and was one of the key policy makers within Portadown Orangeism. Accepting a government appointed place on the Commission was seen by many Orangemen as the ultimate treason. His reasons for joining a body he was once instrumental in trying to destroy are a blend of pragmatism and changed personal circumstances. In July 2005 Burrows separated from his wife and then stepped down as District Master of Portadown. He took his place on the Commission in January 2006 believing he could 'bring something to the decision making process with his particular perspective on the parades issue.' His appointment, and that of another Orangeman Don MacKay, was challenged by nationalists and, following a High Court action, David Burrows was forced to resign from the Orange Order to maintain his position on the Parades Commission.

WON THE BATTLE BUT LOST THE WAR

County Grand Master Denis Watson, when viewing Drumcree 'in the round', doesn't believe there is much to celebrate, 'I think in 1995 the protests were spontaneous. On reflection in 1996, I think the Orange Institution in County Armagh won the battle but that effectively contributed to us subsequently losing the war.'

The Portadown District Orange Lodge website features an Open Letter addressed to the nationalist residents of the Garvaghy Road on 2 July 1998; It was devised as a means for going over the head of the Residents' Coalition leader Breandan MacCionnaith, who is despised by the Portadown Orangemen. The letter is indicative of the mindset of Orangeism in Portadown:

> In a democratic, divided society, accommodation is the only way to build a future where people of differing traditions can peacefully co-exist. Toleration needs to be the approach

when matters of tradition and heritage are expressed. While much of Gaelic and nationalist culture is politicised, the unionist community does not go out of its way to be offended or obstructive. We may not identify with Gaelic and nationalist culture, but we do not attempt to censure it. All we ask for is the same in return for our Protestant heritage and unionist identity.

Breandan MacCionnaith says the Portadown lodges' needle is still stuck on the 'march first; solve everything afterwards' groove,

> They don't see the parade as a problem, but they just have to look at the growth of population in that end of Portadown in the last ten years. When the lodges last paraded along the Garvaghy Road, the Beeches housing development was only starting to be built, but now it's finished. There are new houses going up along the Drumcree Road, the Dungannon Road and the Moy Road. The Orangemen have to be like ostriches with their heads in the sand if they can't see that these houses are likely to be occupied predominantly by Catholics. That's why they need to reach some sort of agreement now on the outward route to Drumcree, never mind the return route.

SINN FÉIN PLOT

Understanding Drumcree doesn't necessarily mean understanding every other contentious parade in Northern Ireland – each has its own distinct local problems. The Orange Order blames Sinn Féin for orchestrating these problems and it is convinced that the Republican Party devised a strategy in the early 1990s to specifically target parades.

Ruth Dudley Edwards's book, *The Faithful Tribe*, a non-fiction portrait of the loyal orders, includes a transcript of a tape-recording which she says was 'secured by a journalist....' on which Gerry Adams is heard telling a Sinn Féin conference in 1997:

> Ask any activist in the north, did Drumcree happen by accident and they will tell you no. Three years of work on the Lower Ormeau Road, Portadown and parts of Fermanagh and Newry, Armagh and Bellaghy and up in Derry. Three years of work went into creating that situation and fair play to those people who put the work in. They are the type of scene changes that we have to focus on and develop and exploit.

The Portadown lodges have been in the Orange vanguard of resisting those 'scene changes'. The District motto is 'Our cause is just – here we stand – we can do no other.' Orangemen have continued to make their stand, at least in token form, on the hill at Drumcree every Sunday since 1998. In the final months of 2006 the Portadown District Lodge told the Parades Commission that it was prepared to enter into a process of mediation without pre-conditions. Taken at face value the statement suggested the Orangemen were prepared to meet the Garvaghy Road Residents' Coalition, which would involve Breandan MacCionnaith. The Portadown Orangemen's spokesperson David Jones was quoted in the

Portadown Times in January 2007 as saying:

> Having consulted with the community and fellow Orange-
> men, we have told the Commission that we're willing to
> enter into mediation and if this leads to face-to-face talks
> then we will participate.

MacCionnaith remains sceptical about the offer, believing the talks would still be conditional on the Orangemen securing a parade down the Garvaghy Road. So far the face- to-face negotiations haven't taken place and such a scenario would have been unthinkable until 26 March 2007 when Ian Paisley astonished everybody by appearing at a press conference, sitting beside Gerry Adams announcing a power sharing deal at Stormont. Now anything is possible.

CHAPTER 5

ORANGE INFLUENCE AT HOME AND ABROAD

The Battle of the Diamond was the spark which lit the Orange torch and the institution, it seems, has been fighting a series of ongoing battles ever since. However, the Order has a military legacy that predates its foundation. Two famous battles dominate Orange culture – the Battle of the Boyne in 1690 and the Battle of the Somme in the First World War. There were numerous other military campaigns in which enlisted Orangemen fought and died, from the 1798 rebellion of the United Irishmen, through the Napoleonic wars, the two World Wars, the Falklands campaign, Desert Storm and the most recent war in Iraq – Operation Iraqi Freedom.

Culturally the most important was the Battle of the Boyne. It was from this confrontation at a river near Drogheda that Orangeism drew its first breath. Following Protestant King William's victory over Catholic King James, Boyne Societies and Orange Clubs were formed in celebration and commemoration. These were the forerunners of the Orange Order.

Having studied the significance of that victory at the Boyne and other battles fought in Ireland at the end of the seventeenth century, Jonathan Mattison says that these battles were 'part of the Glorious Revolution [in England referred to as the 'Bloodless Revolution'] which brought into place constitutional democracy in the British Isles'. He says that there is more of an allegiance to the Glorious Revolution in Ireland because four of its major battles were fought on this island. Many of the old Orange associations and Boyne Societies have their roots in Army Officer Clubs formed after the Williamite Campaign in Europe, and the Battle of the Boyne in particular. Some of the early ideals of the Orange Order stem from that time and the colours – orange and blue – relate to the uniforms and flags of William's army.

William was not a local man but he left an indelible footprint in Ireland during his campaign against the Jacobite forces. As Mattison explains, King William was born into the Nassau family which was originally from the province of l'Orange in France, but later moved to Holland. When William first came to Ireland, and when he fought at the Boyne, he wore an orange silk sash diagonally across his body, from the shoulder to the waist. Until the 1920s, Orange lodges wore a similar sash but they then began to change to collarettes which were cheaper to buy and smaller, making them less cumbersome.

During the 1830s, the Order had a number of lodges connected with military units in the British Army and this created its own problems. Orangeism found itself under increasing pressure when Daniel O'Connell and some radical MPs at Westminster persuaded Parliament to mount an investigation into the institution. As Jonathan Mattison outlines, there was scaremongering that the Order could be used in a *coup d'état*:

> There were lots of Orange lodge warrants issued within the British Army and there was a rumour that the Orangemen were 'an army within the army'. Newspaper reports at that time suggested that the Duke of Cumberland, who was the Orange Grand Master, could call on the services of a hundred thousand serving soldiers within the British Army who were lodge members. That created fear amongst Parliamentarians that the Duke could mount a coup and this led to the 1835 Parliamentary Inquiry into the Orange Institution. Everything about the Order was laid bare. The Orange is continually accused, particularly over the last thirty years, of being a secret society. In reality it hasn't been any such thing since 1835.

Over the decades, new military campaigns were pursued and Orangemen were among those prosecuting the cause on behalf of king and country. The lodges provided an opportunity for fellowship amongst the enlisted brethren and Orange historians say it averted dissention within the ranks. A Grand Lodge report of 1835 states that 'during a strict investigation not a single incident of unsoldierly conduct or want of obedience to military authority could be addressed against them.' When the Orange institution was dissolved in 1836 following a Parliamentary Enquiry, Army headquarters in London sent an urgent order to all the Commanding Officers of Regiments with Orange Lodges in their ranks instructing them that 'all lodges should disband and warrants returned to the issuing authority.'

As with non-military lodges, many resisted and, rather than being returned to the authorities, warrants disappeared into private hands. Some of these military warrants would eventually turn up in the strangest of places after journeying around the world. The Grand Lodge book – Battles Beyond the Boyne – recalls the journey of Warrant number 568 which was issued in 1830 to the 66 Regiment of Foot based at Boyle in County Roscommon. It later became known as Princess Charlotte's Regiment and after almalgamation it was renamed the Beds and Bucks Regiment. The battalion was despatched to Canada in the mid-1830s before moving onto the West Indies by the early part of the following decade. Warrant number 568 next appears in 1846 in a minute book belonging to Lodge 240 in Newtownards in County Down, which records the military lodge having forty-five members and its Worshipful Master being William Elgin who ran a spirit/greengrocers in Mary Street in Newtownards. How the lodge warrant got from Roscommon to Newtownards via North America and the West Indies is still the subject of speculation amongst Orange historians.

There is no doubt that Irish and English regiments carried Orangeism around the world, sometimes literally in their pockets. Orange records refer to an incident during the Battle of Balaclava in 1854 when a British soldier, who was also an Orangeman, was helping to remove the dead and wounded after the disastrous charge of the Light Brigade. He came across a thief stealing a parchment from one of the bodies. He stopped the thief and retrieved the piece of paper which he immediately recognised as an Orange lodge warrant which the cavalryman, who was Worshipful Master of his lodge in Belfast, had been carrying into battle.

There are reports of some British Army regiments forming Orange lodges during the Boer War in South Africa in 1899. It was during this campaign that a young Lieutenant from Belfast serving with the 46˙ Company of Imperial Yeomanry distinquished himself. Orangeman James Craig would later become Viscount Craigavon and Northern Ireland's first Prime Minister. In 1904 Craig presented Ballydonnell Loyal Orange Lodge 1446 in County Down with a flag captured during the Boer War. It was an Orange Free State flag and it bore the inscription, 'This flag was captured from the Boers at Kroonstad, Orange River Colony, on the advance of Lord Roberts to Pretoria. Presented to Ballydonnell LOL 1446 by Bro Captain James Craig.'

Orangeism was to manifest itself more prominently within the military during the early part of the twentieth century. The formation of army lodges was to become a feature in the trenches of the Somme during the First World War. Among the prized exhibits of memorabilia in Orange museums are the numerous grainy photographs of these 'front line' lodges. The pictures may be in black and white, but the Orange sashes are clearly visible over the khaki uniforms of the men standing in the muddy shell-blasted battle-fields. It's said that many of these units of Ulster fighting men charged the enemy positions and fell under a hail of lead with their Orange collarettes still around their necks. These war lodges were important to the young volunteers who were far from home fighting in a foreign country. It helped to instil feelings of home, of togetherness and belonging, which was some small comfort considering the atrocious conditions they found themselves in. It's not unreasonable to assume that there was also probably an element of the 'Billy boys' about it, as young men bolstered their courage with the memory of King William's 'Orange army' and victory at the Boyne. Orangeism in the midst of conflict provided a ready made *ésprit de corps* and was tolerated by senior military commanders who recognised the positive effect it had on morale in the ranks.

The navy also felt the influence of Orangeism, with sailors setting-up 'floating lodges'. The first British navy casualty of the First World War is listed as being an Orangeman – Ableseaman William George Vincent Williams, an Australian who is reported to have been a member of a lodge in Melbourne.

The Orange/Irish influence continues to this day in certain regiments within the British army. The Irish Guards, the Royal Irish Regiment and their associated T.A. units carry on the tradition of recruiting from both sides of the border in Ireland. In recent years these young fighting men have been engaged in the conflicts in Iraq and Afghanistan. While soldiers no longer don Orange sashes as they prepare to go out on patrol, their billets demonstrate the importance of home and cultural identity when facing danger in a strange land. The walls of their makeshift bases will usually be adorned with an array of emblems, predominantly Union and Ulster flags with the names of their home towns scrawled across them.

You may also spot the occasional Irish tricolour representing those soldiers from the Republic of Ireland fighting in a British uniform. Many of them can trace family ties with a particular regiment going back to the 1914–18 World War when northern Protestants and southern Catholics fought and died on the same side. That generative military connection has engendered a respect within the ranks for each others' traditions that exists to this day and makes the 'Irish' regiments so highly regarded as cohesive and effective fighting units.

THE UVF LINK

Orangeism has a long history of military service, as Mattison explains; 'It was heavily involved in the Home Rule crisis. Indeed it was seen as the engine that drove the resistance to Home Rule in the early part of the twentieth century.'

When the Ulster Volunteer Force was set up in January 1913, many of its members were Orangemen. When it was then transferred, almost in its entirety, into the ranks of the Royal Irish Rifles and other units of the 36 Ulster Division which went off to fight at the Battle of the Somme, 'a considerable proportion of the Orange Institution was killed', as Mattison points out.

Orange historians believe that well over a hundred thousand Orangemen fought in the First World War and several thousand of them were killed. The outbreak of hostilities in 1914 meant that many lodges were unable to meet because they did not have enough members left for a quorum. King William's Defenders lodge in Portadown did not meet from November 1914 until July 1918 and it met in 1918 only because a number of injured brethren were home from the frontlines to recuperate. In the Comber District of County Down, so few were the number of Orangemen left after the others had volunteered for service in the armed forces that all the lodges met as one. It was a similar story in other parts of the country.

The Grand Master of Ireland at the time, Sir James Stronge, said,

It is not for Orangemen to limit their patriotism to service on our shores or to wait until the law compels them to take up arms. It is for us to do our duty betimes and with a good will as citizens of a great united Empire, trusting that God will deliver us from the dangers both foreign and domestic, by which we are now encompassed.

Orange lodges in England were also struggling as many of their members were enlisting, moving their Grand Secretary to report in 1916:

The majority of English Orangemen have enlisted and I am glad to be able to say that the Compulsion Bill has only taken a very small number from our ranks, which proves the loyalty or our men who did not wait to be fetched.

A special fund was set up in England to provide a Bible for each of the troops involved in the fighting in France. One such Bible saved one lucky soldier's life when it stopped a bullet that would almost certainly have killed him.

The English Grand Orange Lodge also began an appeal in October 1916 for a designated hospital ward in Nottingham to treat Ulstermen and Orangemen exclusively. The Ulster Recreation Hut and Orange Ward were officially opened by the Duke of Portland in January of the following year.

The First World War has been described as Orangeism's greatest triumph because of the huge number of volunteers who fought; it was also its heaviest defeat in the number of young members killed.

As Mattison says,

> The 1914–18 World War and the partition of Ireland
> coming within a few years of each other were a double
> blow to the Order. There was a generation lost to lodges at
> this time. The Orange used to have a presence in twenty-
> six counties throughout Ireland. That is now down to
> twelve counties.

That link between military service and the original UVF continued on into the Second World War and was equally strong
during the years of the Troubles.

In 2006, when cities, towns and villages were being deco-
rated for Orange parades, UVF flags could be seen flying
alongside the Union and Ulster flags. The Orange Order agrees
that at a time when the institution is trying to promote family-
friendly Orange festivals, the UVF flags create a perception
problem amongst the wider community.

Mattison points out that the flags are not put up by the
Orange Order and that the Order 'does not endorse paramilita-
rism in any shape or form'. He says that the only flag authorised
to be carried in an Orange Order parade is 'a flag with UVF
battle honours on it'. However, that flag is 'heavily identified
with the original Ulster Volunteer Force, not the modern-day
machination of it'.

He argues that the perception problem 'suits the enemies of
the institution who use it as battering ram against us'. He
continues:

They say that's what we represent, but it's clearly not and we have stated that time and time again. It's the same way the IRA use the Irish tricolour. It is supposed to be the representation of the green for Irish nationalism, white for peace and the orange for the Protestant or reformed faith within Ireland. It's been draped over IRA coffins and heavily used by Sinn Féin/IRA but the media and other outside groups don't seem to be so obsessed with the Irish tricolour being used by a fascist organisation.

Neil Jarman has detected a softening of the image in loyalist areas in preparation for the marching season, although he says that this is dependent upon the level of antagonism and political tension within the Protestant and Catholic areas at the time.

'You see this in Orange communities with the removal of paramilitary murals and flags,' he says.

For more than twenty years, paramilitary groups within the loyalist community tended to expand and to become 'the key element of popular culture and celebrations with their flags, music and murals'. However, he says that in the past few years there has been a noticeable 'reining-in' of that, and people have again started to concentrate on Union flags, Ulster flags and King Billy murals. He has noticed also a change in the nature of the bands and the music played.

'I think there is a realisation within the wider unionist community that the confrontational element is not a complete representation of them,' Jarman continues. 'These changes have been successful because they're being driven from within the loyalist/unionist community rather than from without. The people living in these areas don't respond well to being told what to do by outsiders.'

WE WILL REMEMBER THEM

The first Orangeman to win the Victoria Cross during the First World War was Brother Abraham Acton from Whitehaven in Cumbria, who was a private in the Border Regiment. Two other Orangemen also received the highest military honour: Brother Robert Quigg, from Bushmills in County Antrim, who served with the Royal Irish Rifles, and Brother Robert Hill Hanna, originally from Kilkeel in County Down but who emigrated to Canada.

The sacrifice of all the Orangemen killed during the Great War is marked by an eight-foot-high polished granite memorial at Theipval near the site of the Battle of the Somme. It bears the motif of World Orangeism and the inscription on it reads:

> This memorial is dedicated to the men and women of the Orange Institution worldwide, who at the call of King and country left all that was dear to them, endured hardness, faced danger, and finally passed out of the sight of man by the path of duty and self sacrifice, giving up their own lives that others might live in freedom. Let those who come after see to it that their names be not forgotten.

GLOBAL ORANGEISM

Military service, emigration and church missions were a springboard for Orangeism around the world. There are currently Grand Orange Lodges in Ireland, England, Scotland,

Australia, New Zealand, Canada, the USA, Togo and Ghana.

Great Britain

The spread of Orangeism from Ireland to Scotland and England came about through the association of soldiers fighting in the yeomanry and militia. Enlisted men from England joined Orange lodges in Ireland and then took that home to places like Manchester and Liverpool. In a similar way, the first Orange lodges in Scotland were formed in Ayrshire and eventually spread across the northern part of Great Britain.

Canada

Canada's structure of government is said to be based on the Orange model of Private Lodge, District Lodge, County Lodge and Grand Lodge. Orangeism is regarded as the largest fraternal organisation in Canada where it has been active for more than two hundred years. The founding members were mainly immigrants from Ireland. However, as the Order grew, the membership became more cosmopolitan, with Scottish, English, Polish and other European immigrants joining. The most colourful Orangemen in the world are the North American Mohawk Indians. They have their own lodge and they wear the Orange sash or collarette along with their full traditional ceremonial Mohawk costume and headdress.

The first official Orange Association of Canada was formed in Ontario in 1830, although lodges were in operation before this date. Military lodges were established in Saint John, New Brunswick by army men stationed there. Canada's first Prime Minister in 1867, Sir John McDonald, was an Orangeman, and three other Canadian premiers were also members of the Order. The unofficial National Anthem adopted by English-speaking Canadians – 'The Maple Leaf Forever' – was written by Orangeman Alexander Muir.

The United States of America

In the early part of the nineteenth century, Irish immigrants were responsible for Orange expansion in the United States along the western and eastern seaboards. Ulster immigrants had been arriving in the 'new world' throughout the 1700s, some of them with vivid memories and stories about the Battle of the Boyne. Many of them got off ships that had set sail from Derry and Larne and, because of their peculiar Ulster accent and traditions, they were given the name Scotch-Irish.

Some of the very early settlers who struck out for the American frontier so venerated the memory of King William of Orange that they became known as 'Hillbillies'. To be eligible for membership of an Orange lodge in the United States today, a person must profess the Protestant Christian faith, be a legal permanent resident of the US and be male. Women can also join their own Orange lodges in the US and the structure is similar to that in Ireland. The Loyal Orange Ladies' Institution USA and the Loyal Orange Institution USA are two separate organisations co-operating at local, state and national levels in the planning of conventions, social events and other activities.

Australia and New Zealand

A soldier, Andrew Alexander, of the 50 Queen's Own Regiment, who had an Orange lodge warrant sewn into the lining of his uniform, has been credited with introducing Orangeism to Australia in 1835. Ten years later, his military lodge admitted civilians as members and so began the progress of the Order across that vast country.

Around the same time, Orange lodges were flourishing in New Zealand, as more immigrants brought the institution's ideals and rituals to that part of the world. Its rapid success was marked in the 1870s by the setting up the Grand Lodge of New Zealand and, in 1994, it became the first Orange jurisdiction in the southern hemisphere to host a meeting of the organisation's world governing body, when the Imperial Orange Council met in Auckland.

Africa

The first Orange lodges in West Africa were established in Nigeria in the early part of the twentieth century and spread into Togo and Ghana. Missionaries and military personnel are credited with being the main conduits of Orangeism to these outposts of the British Empire, which was still flourishing and therefore assisting during this period of Orange global expansion.

It would be easy to assume that these overseas Orange lodges operated as pseudo ex-pat clubs in the former colonies; however, in the African countries at least, that would be inaccurate. In Togo and Ghana, the membership is drawn from the indigenous populations. There is nothing ex-patriot about the sight of lodges of black men wearing the familiar Orange regalia and collarettes, parading down a dusty street under a blazing West African sun.

When the British Empire was at its peak, it held sway over more than 450 million people. In the early part of the twentieth century, that accounted for nearly a quarter of the world's population. At that time, it was said with all sincerity that 'the sun never sets on the British Empire'. Eventually it did, but it has still to set on Orangeism in those countries where it secured a cultural foothold. The Orange Order influence on political life, however, in these overseas countries was negligible compared to the sway it held in the corridors of power in Ireland.

THE POLITICS OF ORANGEISM

Since partition, the Orange Order has been regarded as a corner stone of the state of Northern Ireland. Historically, one side of the community has seen that as being to its detriment while the other holds a diametrically opposed view. For more than sixty years, the so-called 'Orange card' has been a factor within politics north of the border. When played, it was a card that could be either a king-maker or a deal-breaker.

The Order's role in the creation of the province and the ascendancy of the Ulster Unionist Party was key. Every prime minister of Northern Ireland since the formation of the state has been a member of the Orange Order. Most leading unionist politicians have also been Orangemen. For decades, Northern Ireland and its government were inextricably linked to Orangeism. The copper-fastening of this 'constitutional arrangement' came from the mouth of Northern Ireland's first Prime Minister, Ulster Unionist leader James Craig. During a parliamentary debate in April 1934, he made the following pronouncement:

I have always said I am an Orangeman first and a politician and member of this Parliament afterwards.... They still boast of Southern Ireland being a Catholic State. All I boast is that we are a Protestant Parliament and a Protestant State.

POLITICAL REVIVAL

Orangeism had not always had it so good. Throughout the previous century, the Order's relationship with the political hierarchy had blown hot and cold. Belfast historian Dr Eamon Phoenix says that the important change politically came after the Home Rule threat of 1885, when Orangeism was 'revitalised and rehabilitated', with 'the respectability' again joining. He cites people like Hugh Montgomery who had previously been against the Order, but in light of the Home Rule question changed his views, and the ex-Liberal MP Edward Saunderson who became a member of the Unionist Party and the Order's Grand Master. He points out that the dates on many Orange halls show that they were built in the mid-1880s, at exactly the start of the Home Rule crisis 'when unionism really organised for the first time in Ulster'. Prior to that, Protestant politics in the north of the island had been divided between Ulster Liberals, Ulster Conservatives and 'a very small Orange faction which was not very respectable and unlikely to win many by-elections because it didn't have the support of the landed interest'.

This support was important because before 1872 and the Secret Ballot Act, working class people had to declare publicly who they were voting for. This happened at polling platforms where the dominance of the landlord was acutely felt. If the tenant or employee did not cast his vote as the landlord or employer indicated, he was leaving himself open to punishment.

However, after 1886, Protestant politics in Ulster changed. According to Phoenix, 'This led to the grassroots revival of Orangeism which was vital. It provided the basis for a popular political movement with an aristocratic/middle-class leadership.'

Political expediency and personal economic considerations all come into play when analysing why people were suddenly prepared to 'cosy up' to the Order in the later part of the 1890s. Phoenix argues that 'saving the Empire' was the main motivation. He says that Ireland was viewed as 'the first chink in the armour' and there was a fear that where Ireland went, India would follow. As he points out, that did actually happen in the twentieth century. In the 1880s, Ireland was seen by 'politically powerful and respectable figures' as 'key to Britain's greatness'. It was essential that Ireland not become independent or semi-independent if the British Empire were to remain intact, and this became the major cause of Conservative politics up until the partition of Ireland in 1921. 'British politics were defined in terms of the Irish question,' Phoenix says.

Throughout this period, the Orange Twelfth parades became an essential focus for popular unionist politics in Ulster and, to some extent, Ireland became the 'template for how political parties defined themselves'.

The Liberals were in favour of Home Rule in Ireland and the Tories were against it; within the Tory party, there was a Unionist/Orange element called the Ulster Party, which was a loose conglomeration of MPs who took the Tory whip.

Eamon Phoenix explains how power was administered at Westminster with the Orangemen pulling on some of the levers, namely the fact that all legislation had to be passed by the House of Lords, where the Tories were in control. Thus, as previously discussed, although Gladstone's second Home Rule Bill got through House the Commons, with the support of nationalist MPs from the Irish Parliamentary Party, it was defeated in the Lords.

The unionists lay back on their laurels and made sure that their political machinery was well oiled, so that if another Home Rule crisis came about they would be able to mobilise the Conservatives and Ulster Orangeism to overcome it. 'When it comes to mobilisation in the late nineteenth and early twentieth century, everything is revitalised through Orangeism,' says Phoenix. 'All the levers of power pass through the Order.'

ULSTER UNIONIST COUNCIL

With the defeat of the Home Rule Bill as its goal, Orangeism was a rallying point and it held unionists together at this time. The Orange mortar was also applied to the formation of the Ulster Unionist Council in 1905, forging a link that would be broken only a century later.

The Council was formally constituted at a meeting in the Ulster Hall, chaired by Colonel James McCalmont, who was the MP for East Antrim and also the Deputy Grand Master of the Grand Orange Lodge of Ireland. The aim of the Council was to form an Ulster union for bringing into line all local Unionist associations in the province of Ulster with a view to consistent and continuous political action, to act as a further connecting link between Ulster Unionists and their parliamentary representatives; to settle in consultation with them the parliamentary policy and to be the medium of expressing Ulster Unionist opinion as current events may from time to time require.

James Craig was among the modernisers in Ulster Unionism at that time and he used the Home Rule crisis to terrify the unionist masses into creating an Ulster Unionist Council of which the Orange Order was to become a major component.

Craig realised that Orangeism was in danger of going down the tubes because of popular unrest over issues such as labour conditions in Belfast in the early 1900s. Industry was booming in the city but housing conditions were atrocious and people worked long hours for low wages. It looked as if Orangeism and unionism were losing touch with their own grassroots in this changing climate of industrialisation and modernisation. The formation of the Ulster Unionist Council was an attempt by Craig to galvanise unionism and reconnect the Protestant people.

The Council was made up of not more than two hundred members, half of them nominated by local Unionist Associations and a quarter by the loyal Order. The top drawer of Orangeism was well represented, including the Grand Master of Ireland, the Earl of Erne, and five Deputy Grand Masters. During the Stormont years (1921–72) the Loyal Orders representation on the Council rose to 138 – 122 from the Grand Lodge of Ireland, ten from the Association of Loyal Orangewomen and six from the Apprentice Boys of Derry.

'Orangeism had been recast again,' says historian Eamon Phoenix. 'The core of the Council was Orange and the

Orangemen had been told that they no longer had to put up with imperious aristocratic leaders. They now had leaders with their finger on the Order's pulse and James Craig was one of them; however, he was singularly uncharismatic.'

Craig had a 'master to man' relationship with the masses and he was a figure of fun for some working-class Belfast trade unionists in particular, as he strolled through the shipyard smoking his pipe and wearing his exquisitely tailored suit and white spats.

'Having said that, he always had a word for everybody and was easy with the patter as he mingled with the employees,' says Phoenix. He explains that Craig identified with the aspirations and the fears of the Protestant people of Ulster. 'He represented in his massive blood features, the soul of Ulster resistance and intransigence but he also represented the respectable face of Orangeism.'

The bowler hat was an Edwardian symbol of respectability and it started to be worn by Orangemen after the formation of the Ulster Unionist Council. Around that time, foremen in Belfast shipyard and major engineering firms also began wearing bowler hats. There was a great respectability attached to being what was known as 'a hat' in the shipyard.

Phoenix says that an overlap between the skilled trades and Orangeism in Belfast shipyard led to an aristocracy of labour. He explains that in Britain this was 'contained within the pro-Labour Party trade union movement but in the north of Ireland all of that is sublimated in Orangeism, amid a sense of defensiveness against the dangers of Home Rule.' The land question had threatened Protestant unity, but 'Home Rule provided a basis and Orangeism a vehicle for pan-Protestant solidarity.'

The 1917 Bolshevik revolution in Russia fuelled fears amongst the unionist leadership in Ireland that working-class consciousness in places like Belfast shipyard and other big engineering firms would eventually lead to a 'red menace'. Some historians believe that Orangeism gave the 'working man' a voice within unionism, which helped to deflect him from any kind of adventure into the left-wing politics that were sweeping across Europe.

OVERWEENING INFLUENCE

As a historian, Eamon Phoenix has read and studied the cabinet papers of that period and he has been struck by the overweening influence which Orangeism had during that fifty-year unionist government at Stormont, in terms of key interventions and delegations and protests to ministers.

He cites the case of the Mater Hospital in Belfast, a Catholic ethos hospital, and explains that in the 1940s and 1950s, the Orange Order tried very hard to prevent it from becoming an NHS hospital. The National Health Service had been established in 1948 and Health Minister Billy Grant gave the Mater a stark choice. 'The hospital was told that it could be either 100 per cent in or 100 per cent out of the Health Service,' Phoenix says.

The Mater proposed a contractual arrangement similar to those agreed with denominational hospitals in Britain, whereby the state bought so many beds in a particular unit. The Stormont government, however, turned down any such arrangement with the Mater, which meant that this hospital in

North Belfast, which had been founded in 1883, was refused hospital status. Phoenix points out the irony of the fact that, for the next thirty years, anyone on the nearby Protestant Shankill Road who was seriously injured was rushed to the casualty department of the Mater – a hospital that did not exist.

This is one example of what he describes as 'the insidious and negative influence of the Orange Order throughout the years of the Stormont regime'.

POLITICAL CASUALTIES

The regime also saw several political casualties. Lord Londonderry, described as a man of much broader vision than the average provincial politician, saw a non-sectarian education system as the key to a more united society in Northern Ireland. When his Education Plan was totally destroyed by the Orange influence at Stormont, he opted out of Northern Ireland politics and became a minister at Westminster instead.

The liberal unionist Major Hall Thompson was another casualty in 1949, when, as Minister of Education, he re-organised the schools along the same lines as education in England and increased the grants to Catholic schools to 65 per cent; he was forced to resign. The saddest moment came in 1963 with the arrival of the new-broom unionist Prime Minister at Stormont, Terence O'Neill.

Phoenix says that the promise of something new was snuffed out before it really got going:

> For a brief moment there appeared to be the possibility of ongoing dialogue between representatives of the Orange

and the Green communities on an agenda which the nationalists believed was valid. In the end, Orangeism baulked at it. During that period, the Orange Order's political responses tended to be directed very much against anything that gave quarter to the minority community or that leaned towards inclusiveness.

In the early part of the century, the Orange influence had been more aspirational, but by the 1940s, 1950s and 1960s, it was a reality at Stormont. The corridors of power appeared to be dominated by the Orange ethos. Even the independent members of Parliament were affected by the 'brotherly' atmosphere at 'the big house on the hill', where everybody knew everybody through attending the same lodge meetings and Orange gatherings. When Northern Ireland Labour Party politicians held meetings on the Shankill Road, they wore Orange sashes to demonstrate to their supporters that they were still 'loyal'.

During this period, two things happened. Firstly, it was accepted that being a member of the Order was a prerequisite for political success within unionism; and secondly, Orangeism's reputation among nationalists, as being a fomenter of sectarianism, was cemented.

POWER IN THE PARTY

The power of the Orange within the party would come back to haunt one unionist leader in particular some years later. When David Trimble, an Orangeman since the early 1960s, swept into the leadership of the Ulster Unionist Party, he did so off the back of the first Drumcree stand-off.

The real influence was that the overwhelming majority of the adult males active within the Ulster Unionist Party (UUP) were Orangemen. The Orange delegates in the UUP were party stalwarts up until the time when the Order started to become politicised on pro and anti-Good Friday Agreement lines. Until the 1990s, the Order's leadership was dominated by Ulster Unionists like Martin Smyth and Jim Molyneaux. There was also an unspoken assumption that the Order would position itself behind responsible leadership, politically. The leaders of the Order at that time were the backbone of the unionist community in terms of their social standing. You might even say that the Order was establishment in structure, but it was not politically active as such. Some aspects of it were political in a very broad sense, but not party political.

David Trimble denies that the Orange Order was running the Ulster Unionist Party; nevertheless, he was the leader who pressed ahead with moves to break the historic link between his party and the Orange Order.

'When you say "to break the link", you put it in very crude terms,' he says. 'I was never looking to break the link. What I wanted was to remodel the relationship to make it more appropriate for the situation we are in today. I wanted to do this because first of all there is now a multiplicity of unionist parties as opposed to a single party having a relationship with an organisation that shared the same broad objectives, so it was no longer appropriate.'

Trimble says that his real objective was the reform of the internal structure of the party to make it 'clean and democratic'. He believed that the Ulster Unionist council should be composed solely of delegates from UUP branches as Orange delegates 'were a problem for us in terms of the perception and image of the party and a problem too in terms of trying to broaden the base and the appeal of the party'.

Part of Trimble's aim was to attempt to persuade Catholics to vote for the UUP, but he was also seeking to attract pro-union people who were secular in their outlook or who felt embarrassed by the religious associations in political parties in Northern Ireland and preferred to vote for a party that did not appear to be linked to any denomination.

As David Trimble tried to reposition his party amongst the electorate, the removal of the Orange link got caught up in the controversy over the Good Friday Agreement and sharing power with Sinn Féin.

He recalls that after 1998, the leadership of the Orange Order found itself 'in a slightly ambiguous position' and within months moved towards an anti-Agreement stance. What happened next was that 'gradually over the next couple of years the Leadership of the Orange Order started to drop all the party stalwarts who were Orange delegates and replaced them with delegates who were going to follow the Order's leadership line of being anti-Agreement.'

To be an Orange delegate to the Ulster Unionist Council – the party's governing body – you had to be a member of UUP branch as well as being an Orangeman. The pro-Agreement faction within the Party was aware that the anti-Agreement members of the Ulster Unionist Council were getting their supporters to join UUP branches to load the bases at the Ulster Unionist Council.

'They were effectively stacking the deck within the Ulster Unionist Council and that is the one point at which the Orange Order was being used politically,' says Lord Trimble. 'People were asking, "Why is Trimble continuing when he gets a vote of 53 per cent or 54 per cent at the Council meetings? How could he run a party on that basis?" I knew if you stripped out the Orange vote, then my vote was between 60 and 70 per cent. I knew that amongst the activists of the UUP my true position was in the mid- to high 60s.'

There was very little that David Trimble could do about it at the time. To change the rules of the party required a two-thirds majority and he knew that he had no chance of achieving that. The restructuring and reforms within the Ulster Unionist Party came when the Orange Order broke the link and withdrew its delegates.

Trimble, who is still an Orangeman, says that he does not feel let down by the Order and his fellow brethren, explaining that it was 'a question of what was happening at the leadership level of the Order'. He sees a problem with the current leadership but points out that while some people have left the Orange Order over leadership issues, he knows many who, although they are not comfortable with what the leadership is doing, are intent on remaining within the Order.

Many observers attributed David Trimble's meteoric rise to the leadership of the UUP to his high profile in negotiating a parade down the Garvaghy Road after the first stand-off in 1995. Television news footage showed the local MP wearing his Orange sash walking up and down the paths in the graveyard at Drumcree church, directing the Orangemen and, at times, it seemed, trying to direct the security forces as well.

Lord Trimble, however, believes that Drumcree worked against him in the race for the leadership.

'They did not want a leader who might be seen as being close to Ian Paisley,' he says. 'So that walk down Carleton Street was highly negative for me.' He admits that it may have garnered some Orange support for him 'in the wider unionist family' but says that it did not go down well with the Ulster Unionist Council delegates, who were the people who were going to elect the leader. 'Drumcree did not secure the leadership of the party for me,' he states categorically. 'If Drumcree helped me, it helped in the sense of showing that faced with a challenge, I accepted the challenge and was prepared to approach it, but not in a "safety first" way.' He compares himself with his predecessor, Jim Molyneaux, who he says was 'always safety first, no risking taking and not ... prepared to actually stretch himself on some things', ultimately conceding that Drumcree helped him 'in a round-about way'.

MULTI-PARTY ORDER

Orangeism nowadays is a much more multi-party organisation with all strands of unionism represented within its ranks. While this gives the institution a wider geographical spread politically, it means that its influence on any one particular party is probably less that it has been since the formation of the Order.

Neil Jarman of the Institute for Conflict Research says that despite a fall-off in political influence at the highest level, the institution is still a force to be reckoned with:

As a mainly working-class organisation, the Order can

mobilise support within working-class Protestant communities, and politicians need that support and so want to be associated with the organisation.

However, he believes that 'we've moved away from the time when the Orange was potentially a kingmaker'.

The importance of membership of the Order now is evident mainly, he says, 'when it comes to internal rows over who is the most loyal within the unionist community'. Its power to make and break is now 'confined to local communities' and no longer extends to wider politics. He also points out that 'there's probably no other organisation that has 10,000 to 20,000 members – therefore it's still an important constituency.'

Orangeism and Orangemen have left their mark on politics in Ireland before and after partition. The institution no longer carries the clout it once did but the organisation is still a powerful lobby group and, as we have seen in recent months and years, it can still open the door to prime ministers, presidents and church leaders. Its politics during the heyday of Stormont reinforced sectarian divisions and it can be argued that Orangeism militated against an inclusive approach to Northern Ireland politics because cabinet ministers were constantly looking over their shoulders at the Orangemen who could undermine their political careers. One historian believes that Orangeism's lasting political legacy was put in place before power was devolved to Stormont.

'If the Orange Order hadn't been there during that Home Rule period … you may not have had partition in Ireland,' says Eamon Phoenix, claiming that that was probably the period when Orangeism played its key role. He argues that, after partition, 'the Twelfth was really about celebrating a Protestant state for a Protestant people', and this explains the very close association between the unionist political elite and the Orange Order. However, he believes that over the past thirty years, the Order has gone in a different direction by becoming 'much more working class, much less supported by the middle-of-the-road, middle-class elements within the Protestant community, particularly amongst the business elite'.

'I think the key Orange element in terms of determining Northern Ireland's fate was probably in the early twentieth century,' he concludes.

CHAPTER 6

THE ORANGEMAN AND THE REPUBLICAN

Ask anybody in Ireland and it's likely that they will have an opinion on the Orange Order. The organisation has always attracted a wide range of views, from being held in the highest regard to being held up to ridicule.

This chapter focuses on the thoughts of one particular Orangeman and one republican.

The unnamed Orangeman does not hold high office within the Order and would see himself as a rank-and-filer, a typically ordinary member. He is not a radical, but he and other similarly minded members have voiced feelings of discontent about aspects of the institution. He agreed to be interviewed as an exercise to 'get inside the head of an ordinary Orangeman'. His anonymity has nothing to do with personal security. Rather, it is to allow him to speak freely on sensitive Orange issues, without fear of sanction from within. The author agreed that in pursuit of as candid a viewpoint as possible, anonymity was the best option. This in itself goes some way to explaining the varying levels of unease that still exist within the membership of the Order.

Gerry Kelly MLA (Member of the Legislative Assembly) is a leading member of Sinn Féin, the political wing of the IRA. He is a convicted IRA bomber, who escaped from the H Blocks during the 1983 mass breakout from the Maze prison. He was captured three years later in the Netherlands and was eventually extradited back to the UK. A member of Sinn Féin's Ard Chomhairle (National Executive), he has been the party's spokesperson on Policing and Criminal Justice and in April 2007 became a Junior Minister in the Office of the First and Deputy First Minister at the Stormont Assembly after Ian Paisley's Democratic Unionist Party (DUP) agreed power-sharing with republicans. Gerry Kelly has been at the forefront of nationalist opposition to Orange parades in his North Belfast constituency.

THE ORANGEMAN'S VIEW

From the late 1950s until the mid-1960s my family lived in the 'Holy Land' just off the Ormeau Road in south Belfast. It is here that my earliest recollections of the Orange Order originate. Some time around 1958, I was standing with my parents and older brother outside the Apollo Cinema near the Ormeau Bridge. We were waiting for Ballynafeigh District Lodge to parade from their Orange Hall to the centre of Belfast on a Twelfth of July morning. [At this time, the 'contentious' Ballynafeigh Orange parade and the Lower Ormeau Concerned Community's opposition to it, were decades away.] *What I remember most, however, was not the Orangemen, but rather the sights and sounds of the different bands, dressed in colourful uniforms of orange, purple, red, white and blue. The range of tunes being played blended into a cacophony of noise, including flute and fife, silver and brass, pipes and accordion, and the thumping beat of bass and side-drums. The band leaders exhibited their skills by twirling and throwing the mace or baton high into the air while the spectators watched with anticipation to see if they would catch it on its return to earth.*

The Orange Lodge banners were fluttering in the breeze. They were painted with images from Bible stories, while others depicted state and crown. The most common were portraits of the Duke of Schomberg and of course King Billy, usually but not always, on a White Horse crossing the Boyne. Following the bands and banners came the Orangemen: smartly dressed, many topped off with bowler hats and white gloves, all wearing Orange or Purple sashes or collarettes, some with medals from the First and Second World Wars pinned onto them. Selected lodge members carried flags, others carried deacon poles or highly polished ceremonial swords, which glinted like the war medals in the summer sunshine.

The biggest surprise and delight for myself and my brother was recognising some of the Orangemen. There were people like Mr Cowan who lived opposite us, or Tommy the Co-op bread-server who delivered the bakery products in our area. It was sheer delight when they waved back as we called out their names as they paraded past.

Afterwards, it was a short walk for the family through Botanic Gardens to the Lisburn Road where we sat on the kerbside to watch the 'big parade'. This was the main Belfast Twelfth of July demonstration, when all the Belfast Districts joined up and snaked their way through the city centre in the direction of that mysterious place called the 'Field'. The parade seemed to take hours to pass. The spectacle of noise and colour made such an impression on me that it remains in my mind's eye to this day, alongside other childhood memories such as a first day at school or a particular birthday party.

THE POLITICS OF PARADES

The rationale of parading meant nothing to me. As a six-year-old boy, a parade was a parade. It was similar to that other spectacle that took place annually along the Ormeau Road, the Lord Mayor's Show. As the years passed and particularly after starting school, where the symbols of Britishness were prominently displayed in the assembly hall, I soon learned, in a limited sense, to understand the significance and the politics of Orange parades, the Twelfth of July, and the eleventh night bonfires. As a child, perhaps it didn't register, but there didn't seem to be the same level of tension or antagonism over parades as there is today. The memories I have of the Twelfth up until 1966 were of fun, enjoyment, a sense of occasion and a family day out.

We moved to England and it was five years before I witnessed another Twelfth. By this time, Northern Ireland had literally exploded, although the Troubles had yet to reach their most violent stage. I recall the first Twelfth parade I attended after returning home. I went to the same spot on the Lisburn Road where for so many years as a young boy I'd enjoyed the spectacle. The transformation in five years was unbelievable. You could sense the change in atmosphere. Tension and fear were palpable. The language had changed too. Phrases like 'flashpoint areas', 'no-go areas', 'sectarian bigots' and 'coat-trailers' were being bandied about. I found it difficult to reconcile this language with the decent upright people I knew, like our neighbour Mr Cowan or Tommy the bread-man. As a consequence, I did not attend another Twelfth of July parade for many years after that. Not because I held the Orange Order responsible for the problems of Northern Ireland – I considered myself a unionist, albeit with a small 'u' – but rather, the magic that the Twelfth once held for me as a child had disappeared.

JOINING THE BROTHERHOOD

Within the Orange Institution I am what you could describe as a late starter. I was thirty-one years of age when I joined the Order. In the intervening years, I'd finished my apprenticeship, got married and, along with my wife, had set up a home for ourselves and our children.

My interest in the Orange Order had been re-kindled by my father-in-law. I was somewhat surprised to discover that he was a member of the Orange Institution. He'd joined a Belfast lodge that met in Clifton Street

Orange Hall near the Shankill Road where he was born. Although he now lived about twenty miles outside Belfast, in a rural part of County Down, he still attended his lodge several times a year. My father-in-law, however, never took part in the Belfast Twelfth parade because of the Troubles. Nevertheless, in his own reminiscences of parades past, it was quite clear that he held the Orange Institution in high esteem. One time in the early 1970s he told me that in spite of all the criticism of it, 'the Orange Order can only make you a better person, not a worse one'.

Those words remained with me and I believe they still hold true today for the vast majority of Orangemen. Coincidentally, at the time my father-in-law made that remark, the local District lodge, in the town where I lived, was hosting the Twelfth demonstration that year. On the morning of the parade, my senses were attuned to the sounds of the unseen bands as they arrived at the assembly field on the other side of town. The hairs on the back of my neck stood up as memories of that 'first' Twelfth in south Belfast came flooding back.

In subsequent years, my wife and I attended the various venues that hosted the Twelfth in the rural part of the country we lived in. There was a marked difference between the country and Belfast Orange parades. The country demonstrations were more relaxed. There wasn't the same tension as in Belfast and you felt safe because the townlands and their inhabitants warmly welcomed the brethren and their families. When our children were

*born and began growing up, they too enjoyed the sense of
occasion and the family atmosphere that such an event
generated.*

IN THE SPOTLIGHT

*As the years passed, the Orange Institution became more
and more the focus of attention. Yes, there were times that
focus was to some degree justified. Some rogue elements
within the institution did let it down. Nevertheless, it's
important to put the criticism into context. Here was an
organisation that was being pilloried by the great and the
good, the media, opinion formers, and politicians locally
and internationally, particularly the United States of
America. Yet the majority of the institution's members
were just ordinary folk, men that I worked with, attended
church with and met nearly every day of the week. They
took the insults and the abuse, resigned to the view that
while everybody else was wrong in their opinion of the
Order, nothing Orangemen could say or do would make
them think any differently. Stoicism is a word that readily
comes to mind. It describes my reasoning for joining the
Orange Institution. I saw it as an act of solidarity against
the drip-feed erosion of our British cultural identity.
There was a view around that period, in the early 1980s,
that if the back of the Orange Order could be broken, the
whole unionist family would collapse.*

*I came to realise, that even as a small 'u' unionist, I
had sat on the fence for too long. Little did I realise then
that a series of significant events was about to unfold,*

beginning with the signing of the Anglo-Irish Agreement in 1985. The Orange Institution over the next ten years was to suffer the greatest crisis of confidence since its formation. That particular decade began on a massive high for the Order, in November 1985, when hundreds of thousands attended a rally against the Anglo-Irish Agreement at the Belfast City Hall, and plunged to its lowest point in July 1996 at Drumcree.

PROUD TO BE AN ORANGEMAN

In spite of the adverse publicity attributed to the Orange Institution over the parading issue, I am proud that I am an Orangeman. Not proud in a superior or arrogant way, but proud of the unassuming nature of Orangeism that goes unrecognised. The Christian witness and humility of many Orangemen can be found in the churches where they serve as lay preachers, elders or wardens, and as secretaries and treasurers. In the community and voluntary sector, many Orangemen assist with disabled and elderly people on hospital visits. Some members organise their annual holiday to third world countries to help with the construction of schools and hospitals. They may not be wearing Orange collarettes when they are doing this work, but they are Orangemen all the same.

There are many charities within the Order such as the Lord Enniskillen Orange Orphan Society and the Sir James Clarke Bursary, assisting brethren on low incomes to fund their children in third-level education. The Order also helps charitable institutions outside the Orange family. Pick up a copy of the in-house newspaper, The Orange Standard, *and you will read reports of lodges assisting numerous local and national charities. Many hundreds of thousands of pounds have been raised over the years to help those less fortunate, irrespective of race, colour or creed. The recent Grand Master's Appeal for Cancer Research raised £124,000, which is the largest single donation in Northern Ireland ever made to that body. The Grand Master attributes this quite correctly to the generous nature and charitable outlook of Orange members and their supporters across Northern Ireland and in the border counties of the Republic.*

GOING INTO OFFICE

Within two years of joining the Order, I was elected Lodge Secretary. This job included taking the minutes of monthly lodge meetings, attending to any correspondence, sending out circulars to remind brethren of future events or meetings and forwarding any concerns or issues that needed to be raised to a superior lodge such as the District or County. The bureaucracy of the institution also required the completion of annual returns. As a lodge officer, you are also expected to attend District lodge meetings and to report the proceedings of those meetings to your private lodge.

I also served as District Secretary and although the District Lodge would meet only quarterly, the responsibility was greater, particularly when hosting the Twelfth parade for all the private lodges in that area. The District Lodge office automatically entitles you to membership and voting rights at the County Grand Lodge. It was at this level that I realised just how outdated and cumbersome the structures were within the institution, but also how out of touch the leadership was with the grassroots membership.

JOB SATISFACTION

The fraternal nature of the Order means solidarity and friendships are formed attending social functions or special meetings for the benefit and advancement of the institution. Having held office, there is also the satisfaction of assisting the Orange Institution at a local level with whatever talents that I possess – whether it is the organisational skills of paperwork in all its secretarial forms or helping to organise Orange parades, including the logistical nightmare of major Twelfth demonstrations.

The reward comes when a big parade passes off without a hitch and there's that feel-good factor of knowing that through teamwork the participants and the spectators had an enjoyable day.

There is also a sense of satisfaction that, in some small way, I have been able to influence changes within the institution at a higher level, to bring it into the twenty-first century. Moving the institution forward continues to be a personal challenge, and, although at times it may seem as one 'crying in the wilderness', there are some people taking note. The most important aspect, however, is knowing that my Christian beliefs and my membership of the Orange Order complement one another in bringing the Word of God to an ever-increasingly secular and materialistic society.

ORANGEISM IN SOCIETY TODAY

To understand what role Orangeism has in the twenty-first century, it is worthwhile understanding its role in the past. There is no denying that throughout the history of Ireland and in particular since the formation of Northern Ireland, the Orange Order has provided a sense of safety and stability for many in the Protestant community in Northern Ireland.

From its humble beginnings in the townland of Loughgall after the agrarian conflict at the Battle of the Diamond in 1795, the Orange Order quickly established itself into a local defensive organisation. Within three years, the new Orange Order had spread throughout Ireland and thousands of Orangemen sided with the Crown in suppressing the 1798 Rebellion.

As the nineteenth century progressed, the Order's religious importance as a defender of the Reformed Faith developed, and it remains, to this day, first and foremost a religious organisation. The opening lines of the Orange Order's Constitution read:

The Institution is composed of Protestants, united and resolved to the utmost of their power to support and defend the rightful Sovereign, the Protestant

Religion, the Laws of the Realm ... and will not admit into its brotherhood persons whom an intolerant spirit leads to persecute, injure, or upbraid any person on account of his religious opinions.

Of course, the institution has never divorced itself entirely from politics as evidenced by its part during the various Home Rule crises of the late nineteenth and early twentieth centuries. The Orange Order, for instance, instigated the political formation of the Ulster Unionist Council and was the prime mover behind the formation of the Ulster Volunteer Force to defend the right to remain part of the United Kingdom. In the aftermath of the First World War and the formation of Northern Ireland in 1921, the Orange Order provided a sense of cultural identity in the new political arrangement, in the face of a hostile neighbour in the south. That continued throughout the years of the Troubles in Northern Ireland, when the Orange was looked upon, especially in the border counties, as a bulwark against rampant republicanism.

During the years of conflict in Northern Ireland, the basis of the institution came under intense debate, internally and externally. Was it a political or a religious organisation? The debate intensified in the early 1980s when politicians called upon the unionist people to protest against Dublin interference and the subsequent Anglo–Irish Agreement of 1985. The Orange Order had a ready-made network at local level to organise the protest rally at Belfast City Hall in November 1985. It was one of the largest ever protests in Northern Ireland's history, but the 200,000 strong crowds failed to make any impression upon the British government. Protests marking the first anniversary of the Agreement also failed to make an impact. The great organisation that is the Orange Order had seen its power as a defender of the Union, diminished. The Ulster Unionist Party's support for the Good Friday Agreement was the beginning of the end for the link between the UUP and the Orange Order. The final break came in March 2005.

Along with many other rank-and-file Orangemen, I campaigned for that break with the Ulster Unionist Party, because the Orange Order was not representative of one unionist political party. It's been claimed that the UUP was held to ransom by the 'Orange Card'. If truth be told, the Orange Institution had little influence on UUP policy. In fact, many District lodges didn't bother to nominate representatives to the Ulster Unionist Council. [Orange representation on the Ulster Unionist Council was not automatic; they had to be paid-up members of the UUP before they could be nominated.]

YOU'RE ALL SECTARIAN BIGOTS!

Republicans are amongst the Order's harshest critics. 'Sectarian bigots' and 'coat-trailers' are words often used against us. However, I feel this terminology says more about republicans than Orangemen. It highlights their ignorance of what the Orange Order stands for. Orangemen do not intentionally organise parades to give offence.

But republicans intentionally organise to be offended.

Most of the parades are along established routes that are usually main thoroughfares consisting of commercial premises with a few residential houses dotted along the way. We therefore have to ask, 'Does society want exclusion zones where areas are designated to a certain class of people?' I think the social engineering of apartheid in South Africa answers that question. I would concede that demographic changes occur but when does a tradition begin or end? Does that give anyone the right to deny any group their civil liberties? Millions upon millions have died in two world wars to uphold those liberties in a free society with free speech.

The accusations that Orangeism is a secret organisation that is anti-Roman Catholic is so ridiculous that many of us will not even lower ourselves to get into such an argument. Orangemen are not, as some republicans would have you believe, a sort of supremacist group like the Ku Klux Klan. Orangemen do not operate secretly or wear strange garments with eyeholes cut out of a big pointed hat. We are not a secret organisation as we parade openly for everyone to see and we are easily identifiable because we normally wear bright orange or purple collarettes. Some members even wear bowler hats and white gloves to make them more conspicuous. We do not meet as part of a grand conspiracy to overthrow the Roman Catholic Church, and our halls are open to the public.

There are no oaths, only statements or qualifications. These are neither inflammatory nor illegal when viewed by anyone with a bit of common sense. Our rituals are biblically based and could never be construed as evil. Moreover, all our rituals are in print and open for anyone to view. Minutes of all Orange lodge meetings are open to inspection by the legal authorities. We do have 'secret' passwords which are requested from brethren when opening a lodge meeting, or if a brother is late arriving for a meeting, he gives the password in order to gain admission. There are only two passwords, but more often than not, brethren forget them and, when asked for one or the other, usually mutter something unintelligible. Curiously 'Fish and Chips' is a common password.

I feel a lot of the myths and slogans offered by republicans to their own community are about instilling fear and making the Orange Order out to be something that it's not.

THE ORANGE AND VIOLENCE

Throughout its history, some Orange parades have been involved in controversy. The most famous incident was at Dolly's Brae near Castlewellan in 1849. I watch with wry amusement when an Orangeman sings the song 'Dolly's Brae' with gusto as if it were a great victory. Without going into who was 'right' or 'wrong', it was in fact a disaster for the Orange Institution. It brought about the Party Processions Act of 1850 that banned Orange parades.

There are similarities with the original Drumcree protest of 1995. At the time, many brethren, myself included, saw it is a principled stand and a great victory for the

Orangemen, but it was a hollow victory.

The Unionist people had, over the previous decades, perceived the diminution of their British identity. Remember the phrase 'no selfish, strategic or economic interest by Britain in Northern Ireland' uttered by the then Secretary of State Peter Brooke in November 1990? Confidence and morale within the Unionist/Protestant community were at an all-time low. There is no doubt that the Orange Order fell hook, line and sinker for the Sinn Féin orchestrated targeting of parades that was starting to take shape throughout Northern Ireland in that period. We knew it then, but our dogged determination and sense of hurt were only aggravated by this knowledge. As a unionist people, we had 'rubbed out the line in the sand' so often that this was a line too far, and this time the Orange Order was prepared to make a stand. Orangemen are slow learners and seldom look to their own history to see the mistakes that were made in the past.

We know what happened because of the Drumcree protest. There is no forgiving the rioting, the damage, devastation and disruption it caused, despite the Orange Order's appeal for calm. While Orangemen took part in the rioting, the vast majority of members didn't get involved and deplored the violence. Most of the violence was committed by the paramilitaries who had their own agenda. Of all the images of Drumcree, the one that did us the most damage was David Trimble and Ian Paisley walking through lines of Orangemen in the centre of

Portadown with their hands clasped in a triumphant salute. The politicians had used the Orange Order once again and I personally believe that David Trimble secured the leadership of the Ulster Unionist Party through his participation at Drumcree. He became an Orange hero. How the mighty have fallen.

The aftermath of Drumcree tore the institution apart. I attended many meetings at County and Grand Lodge level that were acrimonious, verbally volatile and ended in discord. Much of the debate focused on 'obeying the law of the civil authority' as written into our constitution. It did the Orange Order irreparable damage, with many hundreds leaving the institution at all levels. Today we are still feeling the aftershocks and witnessing the fallout from Drumcree at other parade venues like the Lower Ormeau, Whiterock and Springfield Roads.

The debate continues within the institution about which road to travel in the future. I believe the Orange Order must engage with those who disagree with it, just as unionist politicians have done. We have articulate people within the Order who are able to put forward a just argument for the right to parade that no one can disagree with. We need to inform public opinion of the true nature of the opposition to the Orange institution. In my view, it's the opposition not the institution that's based on sectarian bigotry and republican coat-trailing exercises.

PARADING AND BAD PUBLICITY

Countries throughout the world celebrate their identity

and culture through parades. France has Bastille Day, the USA has Independence Day and Brazil has the carnival in Rio de Janeiro. In England, the Notting Hill Carnival, which grew from humble beginnings, has become one of the largest street parties in Europe. I feel the Orange Institution is no different in celebrating its cultural identity.

Some brethren believe the institution is just about parading on 12 July, for others it's an all-year-round commitment in which the Twelfth celebrations are the culmination. Many Orangemen prefer attending church parades as a public witness to their Reformed Faith but in whatever context parading is placed, it has an important role in reflecting 'who we are and what we stand for'.

This brings to the surface a problem that has dogged the Order since it began. It has never succeeded in getting its message across to the wider community and beyond. One of the main criticisms at grassroots level is the institution's ineffectiveness when dealing with the media. With modern communications and instant globalisation of news and current affairs, the Orange leadership has failed abysmally in communicating its message. There has always been a fear of engaging with the media. As I said earlier, 'stoicism' seems to be the watchword of the institution and there is great mistrust of the media generally. Within Orangeism, many see journalists as the enemy because they don't always reflect the truth and are always trying to trick an interviewee into answering questions that suit their own agenda.

Although it is easy to criticise the leadership on their communication skills, it's not all their fault. They're not properly trained to engage with the various types of media they encounter and the 'clever' journalists among them. There is another problem contained within Law 10 of the Constitution of the Orange Order, which is in effect a gagging order. It deems that only the Grand Master or other high-ranking officials are permitted to speak on major issues. We have articulate brethren within the institution, but unfortunately, until the present archaic structure is changed and they are allowed to speak out, the present leadership will be seen to be bumbling and inept.

[To add context to this argument, it should be noted that the Orange Order has failed spectacularly at times in its dealings with the media. It could be argued that the die was cast on the day when Robert Saulters was elected Grand Master in 1996. During his first press conference at Orange Headquarters in Belfast, he rounded on the Labour leader Tony Blair. He repeated some of the remarks he had made a few months earlier on the Twelfth of July when he had referred to the future British Prime Minister as 'a turncoat' who had 'sold his Protestant birthright by marrying a Romanist and serving communion in a Roman Catholic Church'. This direct and personal attack on Mr Blair and his Catholic wife, Cherie, by the new Grand Master astonished many of the media representatives present.

There were numerous other incidents. Infamously during a contested Orange parade through the mainly nationalist Lower Ormeau Road in 1992 following the sectarian murder of five people in Sean Graham's bookmaker's shop, by the loyalist paramilitary group the Ulster Freedom Fighters, television news pictures clearly showed several Orangemen triumphantly holding up their white-gloved hands, displaying five fingers to the nationalist crowds watching from behind the security cordon near the bookmaker's shop. The Orangemen who were identified as being those who made the obscene 'five fingers' gesture were later disciplined by the Order but it was done on the quiet 'within lodge'.

During the worst of the loyalist/unionist/Orange violence arising from the Drumcree stand-off, the then District Master of Portadown, Harold Gracey, refused to condemn it. When pressed as to why he refused, his response was that Gerry Adams – the Sinn Féin leader – never condemned IRA/republican violence.

Throughout the Drumcree dispute, Portadown District Lodge looked after its own PR. Local Orangeman David Jones was the first point of contact and his republican counterpart was the Garvaghy Road Residents' Coalition spokesman Breandán MacCionnaith. David Jones was faced with defending consecutive nights of rioting at the security barrier at Drumcree, when Orangemen and loyalist paramilitaries attacked the police and army. Breandán MacCionnaith, meanwhile, less than a quarter of a mile away on the peaceful Garvaghy Road, was explaining to the world's media how the nationalists were suffering because of the 'ring of steel' security operation put in place to protect them from the Orangemen. If King Billy had been galloping past on his horse, blindfolded, he would have seen who was winning and who was losing the propaganda war.

More recently, after the 2005 Whiterock Orange parade in West Belfast, the city witnessed some of the worst street violence it had seen for years. The police and army came under sustained and clearly planned attack from loyalist rioters with Orangemen amongst them. Petrol bombs and stones were thrown and, at one point, shots were fired at the security forces. In a press conference some days after the trouble, the County Grand Master of Belfast, Dawson Bailie, tried to explain what had happened by blaming everyone but the Orangemen and their supporters.

In the mid- to late-1990s, media liaison officers were appointed by some other District lodges, most notably Ballynafeigh in Belfast's Ormeau area. These officers found themselves trying to promote the more positive elements of the Order, such as charity collections and cultural evenings, at a time when street violence, turmoil and intransigence had taken hold of the Orange Institution like a vice-grip. They were on a 'hiding to nothing', and very soon their contact telephone numbers were ringing out or no longer available as every call from a member of the media was about the latest controversial parade or riot.

Later, the Grand Lodge employed its own PR team, based in the new Orange Headquarters, Schomberg House in East Belfast. Press releases were sent out, information days and off-the-record press briefings were organised and generally well attended. But once again, when it came to the tricky questions, the leadership was found wanting, usually retreating behind a now-familiar curtain of non-culpability and stoicism. At the end of the 2006 marching season, the Orange Institution took another step out into the media abyss with the appointment of a new press and public relations manager, Austin Hunter. A well-known journalist and public relations executive, Hunter has worked as a news reporter for the BBC, was Head of Public Relations with the RUC/PSNI and latterly was a senior editorial executive with the *Belfast Newsletter*. He is by far the most accomplished media person to hold the PR post at Orange Order Headquarters. It is too soon to judge what impact, if any, he will have on getting the Orange message across. The urgency of winning the public relations battle is not lost on many rank-and-file Orangemen.]

TIME FOR CHANGE?

When it comes to Orange-related issues, the media's main focus, of course, is on the marching issue. In my opinion, the majority of 'grassroots' Orangemen are opposed to Grand Lodge's policy of not talking to the Parades Commission or certain residents' groups. There's a feeling that the leadership are like ostriches, sticking their heads in the sand and hoping the problems will resolve themselves. Moreover, there is a groundswell of opinion that where parades are in dispute, then those who are affected should be permitted to engage either through direct dialogue or by proxy to resolve the situation locally. As it stands, no lodge ,whether at private or District level, can oppose the present Grand Lodge ruling preventing this happening. If they do, there's the possibility of losing their warrant and being expelled from the Order.

It may not be noticeable outside the institution, but there have been some minor alterations in its structure over the last few years. The call for change came from the private lodges who were constantly frustrated at Grand Lodge's antiquated hierarchical system. This system is based on the pyramid structure where those few at the apex are able to impose their authority over those at the base level. It is supposed to operate on the principle of representative democracy. Unfortunately, many at the top forget that principle and impose their personal views rather than the views of those they are supposed to represent.

It operates like a cartel or old-boy network, beginning at County level. To be nominated to Grand Lodge, an Orangeman must first reach County Lodge level and it's only those members who demonstrate that they're on the same wavelength as the hierarchy that get nominated. If a person is nominated and there is no other nomination, then that person is automatically elected to that office without a vote. This occurs at all levels of the institution and prevents the institution from progressing. I believe that similarly rigged elections or nominations take place when the Roman Catholic Church nominates its cardinals. The clerical candidates must hold similar doctrines to the incumbent Pope so as to ensure a continuity of doctrinal faith.

We have had some success with the Orange structure where a delegate from each District can now sit on Grand Lodge; however, it still difficult for a private lodge to raise a 'point of issue' at Grand Lodge level. The private lodge must first seek approval from the District lodge. If the District agrees, it is forwarded to the County. If the County agrees, it is forwarded to Grand Lodge. If a private lodge manages to clear both the District and County lodge hurdles and reaches Grand Lodge, it still has to jump the Central Committee fence. If the 'point of issue' raised by the private lodge is not to the liking of Central Committee, it will fall like a donkey at Beecher's Brook. To use a different analogy, one Orangeman described the Central Committee as being like a 'roomful of receptionists ... nothing gets past them'. This procedure of official communication with the Grand Lodge leadership has changed little in two hundred years.

There was some revising of the laws and ordinances a few years ago. Although many of the laws are relevant and necessary, numerous others are well past their sell-by date. Some laws are ignored and others are bent. The one thing I did realise very quickly when I joined the Orange Order is that change comes about very slowly!

UNDERSTANDING ORANGEISM

I believe that most people outside the institution would have some basic concept of what it represents. You need only look at the banners and flags with their symbolism of all that is British. They may also know why Orangemen parade on the Twelfth and how the phraseology of 'civil and religious liberty', 'this we will maintain' are all linked to the Battle of the Boyne in 1690. However, I feel that in the wider historical context, many will not know what Orangeism is all about.

For instance, the Battle of the Boyne was a relatively minor battle in a much wider European conflict. The Glorious Revolution of 1688 was one of the most important historical dates of English history, paving the way for a parliamentary democracy that replaced the divine right of kings to rule. I think there's a tendency for both Protestant and Roman Catholic to look at Orangeism in isolation and only in the context of Ireland.

OUTREACH AT LOCAL LEVEL

Between 1989 and 1996, my own District lodge embarked on an outreach programme, which involved the local community, both Protestant and Roman Catholic. We engaged with state and Roman Catholic schools in a process of reconciliation and mutual understanding. The reasoning for this was quite simple. In our opinion, the government policy at that time of 'education and mutual understanding' was only a cosmetic exercise. Taking children from different religious backgrounds on joint school trips or the twinning of Catholic and Protestant schools was, in our opinion, not addressing the real issues of difference and perception.

We initiated exhibitions and open nights in the local Orange Hall. We went along to schools on both sides of the community at primary and secondary level, giving talks, engaging in debates in a Question Time *format. We covered any aspect of Orangeism and its role in European history of the seventeenth and eighteenth centuries.*

Short-story competitions and art exhibitions were organised for the pupils, and Roman Catholic children along with their parents attended the prize-giving ceremony in the Orange Hall. At the beginning of this exercise, the perception of the Orange Order was stereotypical but by its conclusion many went away with the view that the Orange Order was not the threat they had first assumed. There were some people, however, we could not convince. Unfortunately the advent of Drumcree undid a lot of this good work.

In recent years, despite disputes over a few parades, the ongoing peace process is creating a rethink on how we can and must live together. There are now dozens of District and private lodges that have embarked on Outreach projects, not only to impart understanding but also to understand. Some lodges have open nights with guest speakers from different backgrounds, politically and religiously, in order to progress understanding of one another and to break down the barriers.

IS THE FUTURE ORANGE?

I believe the falling membership in the aftermath of the Drumcree disputes has bottomed out. There are signs that the institution is once again attracting new people from all classes. Most are well educated, and that bodes well for the future in producing new leaders and thinkers. Membership will never again reach the halcyon days of the 1950s and 1960s, but I believe that what we lack in quantity will be replaced by quality. Some brethren are even now discussing replacing a lot of our archaic and

*sometimes emotive language, such as the Twelfth Dem-
onstration with Twelfth Celebration, and parades would
be organised that would involve all the community,
including the ever-growing ethnic minorities.*

*Orangeism's new role in society is still in the embry-
onic stage. It will take a while for us to 'find our feet' after
the break with the political baggage of the past. Politics
will continue to be part of our organisation but only in
our personal and private lives. I can see the Order engaging more with its Christian principles and defending the
Reformed Faith particularly with the encroachment of
ecumenism. I think it will also become more of a
community-based organisation. For example, ten years
ago, a few District lodges in deprived areas decided to set
up their own credit unions. Today there is hardly a District
that does not help in managing a credit union.*

*The Orange Order is set to be around for a long time to
come, although it will not have the same influence in
Northern Ireland society that it once did. Some see this as
a retrograde step; others view it as an advantage.*

*Whatever the outcome, we are hopefully on the road to
a true peace process and while not embracing every
aspect of each other's culture, let us respect it for what it
is, in mutual trust and tolerance.*

THE REPUBLICAN'S VIEW

[Gerry Kelly MLA was interviewed several months before
power sharing was agreed in the new Stormont Assembly and
his subsequent appointment as Junior Minister]

Sinn Féin views the Orange Order as a sectarian organi-
sation. It is anti-Catholic. Its own writings prove that.
Anecdotally, I remember around the time of the Tour of
the North [a contentious Orange parade in North Belfast
which passes through a nationalist area], *Orangemen*
were asked why they felt they had to walk down Clifton-
park Avenue, which was a mile out of their way, to get to
the same place they could have got to by walking down
the Crumlin Road, which is almost entirely Protestant.
They replied that that was part of it – 'the nationalists
need to know that we can walk through their district.'

It obviously has a historical coat-trailing part to it
which goes right back to the time when the landlords
would go through the tenant hovels to show that they
could. Now I say that nearly in isolation because I'm not
sure how many people would be aware of it…. But I'm
not saying necessarily that's what Orangemen are very
aware of. They're clearly aware that it's anti-Catholic, that
it's putting the 'Fenians' in their place. Clearly it's also fed
by the fact that we've come through a very long conflict.

The coat-trailing isn't all anti-republican and this is
where it gets sectarian. It is anti-Catholic, which in a way
is a greater difficulty. You can understand an anti-IRA
stance because the IRA is intent on having a United Ire-
land, on having a different political system from what
was before. But the sectarianism in the Orange is at the
base of it; it's the lowest common denominator. On the
Crumlin Road during the Twelfth of July parade, in an
area where the two communities live close to each other,

where they know each other, you'll see [loyalist] *women dressed up as nuns with fake bare bosoms exposed. This is a clear insult to religion as opposed to republicanism. They can burn effigies or photographs and posters of me until the cows come home, but people get really insulted when you see that type of anti-Catholic thing and when the Rev. Ian Paisley talks about the Pope being the anti-Christ.*

When I was being brought up in a very large Catholic family of eleven children, we would never use the term Roman Catholic. Obviously it does designate that it's Catholic connected to the Pope in Rome but we never had the sense that we had to be very specific about that. We were Catholics or even Irish Catholics, although even that may be confusing because there are other types of Catholics in the Irish Anglican church. But it was never a big identification issue for us and people used to get annoyed when Paisley and others, particularly in the early days, called us Roman Catholics. I remember my mother getting very annoyed that these people were trying to define us as something entirely different.

In the 1960s, I was working as a civil servant in the Northern Ireland Electricity Department. It was a big complex on Belfast's Lagan embankment, with lots of people employed there. I wasn't brought up very political at all, but it was a phenomenon that, two to three weeks before the Twelfth, people starting making sectarian remarks. The same people who'd got on well with me throughout the rest of the year starting making remarks such as 'There's the wee Fenian bastard now' and 'What are you gonna do on the Twelfth ... sure you don't take your holiday?' It was amazing. I'd been told about it, but didn't believe it.

You can only assume that part of it is the environment that some people grow up in. I do remember comments by some Protestants who actually believed that Catholics kept coal in their bath. Part of it is understandable because Fenians are seen as rebels. In any colonial situation or in apartheid South Africa, to dislike someone or to dislike a group of people or even a nation, you have to diminish them in some way. So they become educationally subnormal or they keep coal in the bath; they wash only once every three weeks. You have to be able to dehumanise people to dislike them and it is an environmental and political thing as opposed to somebody being born as a Catholic or a Protestant and automatically hating. A lot of it's accidental. You're accidentally Catholic or accidentally Protestant and it has to be learnt so there is nothing endemic about it.

If I had been born a Protestant, it's quite possible that I would have reacted in the same way. I would like to think, however, that if I reached a certain age I would have had a different view ... I would have been able to make up my own mind and grow out of it or analyse my way out of it. I think I've done that with some parts of my life.

I might have been an Orangeman, for instance. There is a place in your life where you start questioning, and I

*have questioned republicanism, I questioned my religion,
I questioned the things happening around me. I like to
think I have a much wider view of the world. I ended up
in jail in England, which was an education in itself
because it was an entirely different environment. After
that, I was 'on the run' in Europe.*

*I certainly believe now that I'm at a stage, and have
long since been at a stage, where I will make decisions
not based on the way I was brought up or who I was
brought up as, but on the basis of whether I think it's right
or wrong. Now, clearly you don't have that in every individual. Clearly there is an environmental thing going on
and that's where sectarianism comes from.*

There's a book called The Mass Psychology of Fascism,
*which looks at the question of Nazism in Germany and
asks why people there didn't do something about it. Those
are important questions because you have to divide out
the individual and the phenomenon of mass movements
or communities which turn one way or the other. People
talk about polarised communities, but they are polarised
on the basis of a lot of beliefs, many of which are false.*

*Regarding the Orangemen's belief that Sinn Féin
deliberately orchestrated the parades problem, I don't
know about the Gerry Adams quote ,but I presume it's a
misinterpretation because I can see myself in a place like
Ardoyne saying, 'You can't work this problem out, without organising.'*

*We didn't just land up on the Twelfth of July. We talked
to people first and the response was: We're not taking*

these Orange parades any more. We've taken them all along and why should they walk through this area again. Also things shift. At one stage, you had a conflict here, which was almost entirely between the British Army and the IRA. Then you had loyalists involved in sectarianism and, if you take the microcosm of North Belfast, more than two-fifths of all the casualties in the Troubles happened here, so the majority of that was killing Catholics. Those are the atmospherics.

Remember, the Orange Order didn't march through these areas in North Belfast for a long time because of the Troubles and the shootings on both sides of the community. The Tour of the North stopped in the 1970s and it didn't resume until the 1990s. So it became an issue again after people had come through all the rest of what was going on, and when it was reintroduced they were not prepared to accept what they looked upon as coat-trailing.

In terms of the Cliftonpark Avenue parades, I would have held a number of meetings with people in the area but the demand in North Belfast was already there to stop the parade coming through, and the protests on the Cliftonville Road were all passive. I was arrested on one of those protests and beaten and charged by the RUC. It later emerged that the only reason I was charged was because I was the elected representative who everybody knew. There was no strategy on the parades issue as such; that's different from the phenomenon of protests to try to stop parades marching through certain areas. The door had been opened a little bit but there was such a vast hunger for change on this issue that the pressure from within forced it wide open. Historically, once there is movement in a certain direction, you get momentum ... momentum on things which had been niggling at people for years but had no expression ... and it wasn't just in North Belfast; it happened elsewhere. Sinn Féin didn't have to organise it. We did not organise the Drumcree protests; the Garvaghy Road residents did that, but they came to us for help. So we(Sinn Féin) assisted them politically. I understand why it was seen as some sort of a conspiracy but it wasn't.

On a political level, the DUP were saying, 'We will not talk to Sinn Féin ... because they are IRA.' If I try to pick who represents your party, the Orange Order or a residents' group, then I'm in the wrong business. The residents pick who represents them, the electorate selects their political representatives and the Orange Order picks their own people. I may have a massive difficulty with the people who are selected but I have met with members of the UDA at certain times, so it clearly isn't a matter of principle and, in certain circumstances, members of the Orange Order have met republicans ... so if it's not a matter of principle, then it has to be a matter of tactics.

I was in jail and it's quite obvious what my background is so they can say, 'We're not talking to Gerry Kelly.' I can go and get somebody else who has been a Republican all their life, who has never had any profile, but who may have done much more than I have and because the Orange side don't know that, they maybe want to talk to that guy and that's why it's so ludicrous and that's why it's a tactic. The Orangemen didn't want to talk to residents' groups so the excuse became ... they were organised by Republicans.

Overall, I feel there is a great resistance to change within Orangeism and also a great fear. I have no fear of talking to anybody, because I think, and I might be wrong, that, at least in a general sense, my beliefs are things which I can stand over, that I can argue with anybody over.

The Protestant community feed off each other. You have the political parties, the churches, the Orange Order, and they have this general fear of having dialogue, although there are exceptions. The basic concept is that they're against change and they fear dialogue will bring change or lead to compromise. Republicans don't have that fear.

I do take cognisance of the legacy of hurt and loss within the Order over members who've been killed by the IRA and I also understand it. But there's a difference between understanding and excusing. The flip side of that is that members of the Orange Order, members of the UDR, members of the RUC and loyalism in general, have been involved in killing Catholics.

That's the difference between conflict resolution and conflict itself. So it's a fair demand of me and it's a fair question of me: Do you understand that my brother, daughter, son, husband or father was killed by the IRA? Yes, I do have to do that, and I want to do that. But equally, I have also lost loved ones, lost comrades, lost family ... and people need to have a view of that because in conflict resolution that's what counts. That's where I don't think the Orange Order has arrived yet ... again with exceptions because there are exceptions to all of this. You can sort things out with friends, but the real job is sorting it out with your opponents. That's why I knock on the door of British ministers on behalf of my constituents. I accept it would be hard for the Orange Order to do that if I was the Minister in charge. Equally, there will probably be a DUP minister and I despise the [sectarian] *politics of the DUP; however, Ian Paisley, and anybody else who has a mandate, needs the respect of having that mandate so whatever you think of the person, I have no hesitation in going and talking to him to try to work something out.*

In the end, everybody else around the Orange Order, certainly on the nationalist side, is up and ready for this. That doesn't mean to say they're going to roll over and they're going to sort it out at the first meeting. But the lesson to be learnt from elsewhere in the world is that at some point in any conflict, you will end up at the negotiating table.

I keep telling our people there are two ways for a conflict to end – an absolute victory of one side over another or going to the negotiating table. The best thing you can do is get there as quickly as possible. Nationalists are there already and, in my opinion, this is unionism and Orangeism's time too and they need to be talking.

Sinn Féin is not here to wipe out the Orange culture. I understand that fear, but that claim is absolutely not true. It is part of our culture. There's a part of Orangeism that I don't like but I wouldn't be running around pulling down King Billy statues or changing street names ... because they reflect a part of the history of my country, because it's our country so it's part of our history. I mean, I'm well past that; I might have been at that when I was twelve or something.

You have to allow for other people's culture, but you can't allow for racism or sectarianism on either side; you have to take a stand against that. That doesn't mean you start writing books where the Ku Klux Klan never existed. They did exist and it's a part of history that you might read and be appalled at what happened, but you wouldn't tear the page out of the book. That is what affected the next part of history. Sinn Féin doesn't want to do that. We know there's a Britishness, we know that it's part of our history and not just in the last eighty years. If you go right back to the time of the United Irishmen, they were almost entirely Presbyterian and we're proud of that. We didn't want a confessional state; we're proud of the 1916 Proclamation. I think in our own way, we can prove we are not about wiping out the Orange culture.

CHAPTER 7

VIEW FROM THE TOP

Drew Nelson is a solicitor with his own practice in Dromore, County Down. His election as Grand Secretary of the Grand Lodge of Ireland in 2005 made him one of the most influential figures within Orangeism. His appointment may have come as a bolt out of the blue for many Orangemen, but for those in the know, he was always the coming man within the Order.

The forty-nine-year-old former part-time officer in the Ulster Defence Regiment is a Queen's University law graduate. His foray into politics saw him stand unsuccessfully as an Ulster Unionist Party candidate in the Westminster elections of 1992; from 1993–97 he served as a UUP member on Banbridge Council before leaving the UUP in 2004. He was District Master of the Orange Order in his hometown area in the early 1990s. He had appeared in the media occasionally throughout that period, speaking on Orange issues or as an elected representative, but his profile was very much at a local-issues level. Not long before his election as Grand Secretary, he made the Northern Ireland television news and the daily papers when he turned up near Belfast at a public auction of car number plates, and successfully bid for a plate carrying the numerals 1690.

Drew Nelson is viewed as a modernising force within the Order. He is also seen as a clever strategist with a keen political mind. Articulate and affable, he is regarded as a good media performer, an area that has been an Achilles heel of the institution. He has been a driving force in taking the Orange Order down a less 'traditional route'. While at one with the vast majority of Orangemen in wanting to see the demise of the Parades Commission, he also recognises the value of taking the Order's case to people who, just a few years ago, they 'wouldn't have touched with a barge pole'.

Since coming into office, Nelson has been involved with Orange delegations meeting the leader of the Catholic Church in Ireland, the leader of the nationalist SDLP, the Irish government and the President of Ireland. Of course he was not alone in mapping out the way forward. Others at the top end of the Order were also in agreement that the meetings should take place. It is this public demonstration of a willingness to engage in dialogue (something the Parades Commission has been impressing on the Orange Order since it was set up in 1997) that has opened doors and coffers. The British government agreed a £100,000 grant to fund a development officer to promote Orange parades as a tourist attraction in Northern Ireland. This has made some people think that perhaps things are changing within Orangeism and a resolution of the parades issue may be possible. Others see the money as a sop and view the dialogue that has been taking place as cynical politicking by the Order.

In the early summer of 2006, I conducted an interview with

Drew Nelson at Schomberg House in east Belfast, headquarters of the Orange Order. It sheds light on hitherto 'dark areas' and is an indication of the current mindset of those at the apex of the Order as it marches off into the new millennium.

INTERVIEW WITH DREW NELSON

Is the Orange Order sectarian?

The Orange is not a sectarian organisation; it's a denominational organisation. In fact, we are a unifying force amongst Protestants. We have eighteen different Protestant denominations within the membership of the Orange.

A recent survey of the Order's membership (estimated at between 35,000 and 50,000) has thrown up some interesting findings. What are these?

Almost half the Order's membership thinks that the religious aspects are the most important and the other half believes that the cultural aspects are most important. We don't divulge figures on the membership; however, it's about the same as it was in the mid to late 1800s. At that time, there was an increase in people joining with the anti-Home Rule campaign and the formation of the state of Northern Ireland. That membership has very slowly, almost imperceptibly, declined during the last twenty-five years or so. However, we are happy with the present membership in Northern Ireland, which is roughly half the size of the British Army throughout the UK.

There are tens of thousands of Orangemen in Scotland

217

and England as well. In the rest of the world, Orangeism has gone through a decline , but we are now seeing a bit of a resurgence through reorganisation. Orange lodges in Canada have left the city centres and gone seeking their membership in the suburbs where a number of smaller Orange halls and clubs have been constructed. The shift of populations also affects Northern Ireland. The recruitment area for lodges in Belfast city centre is essentially inner city. The lodges in the suburbs now come under the other County lodge areas such as Down and Antrim.

There is no problem keeping the city centre lodges going, we still have a sufficiently high membership in Belfast but it has naturally declined as the Protestant population in the inner-city areas has declined. But it's not a rapid decline in membership.

I think if we are to remain relevant we have to go into the suburbs – not so much the rural areas because they are already served by the rural lodges. But we need to be doing something in the suburbs of Belfast. There are now enormous populations in places like the Belvoir estate, Dundonald, Rathcoole, Newtownabbey, Finaghy and Dunmurry where we haven't really reorganised. That's what the Orange Lodges have done in Toronto and that's something we need to be looking at.

How many Orange halls are there in Ireland?

There are about 750. Almost all of them are north of the border with about thirty halls in the Republic centred mostly in Counties Donegal, Monaghan and Cavan, with one or two in Leitrim and Dublin. Interestingly, we have picked up new members in the Republic over the last couple of years in counties in the midlands and also in Limerick and Cork. I have spoken to these new members and asked them why they decided to join the Order now. One new member from a farming family told me that they always regarded themselves as British, but during the years of the Troubles on the other side of the Irish border, it was just too controversial a thing for him to join an Orange lodge. He said that now that the Troubles have faded he feels more confident about doing it. Another new member said he also felt his Britishness and was fascinated by the Orange Order, but lacked the courage to make contact and join a lodge during the time of conflict in Northern Ireland. Even with this recently acquired confidence, one of the new members revealed that he still hadn't made his family aware that he'd joined the Order.

I think the internet has been a great boon for the Order. We have seen a particular resurgence in the USA and it's all internet-based. I think there's also a lodge just setting up in Poland through the internet which has been issued a warrant by the Grand Orange Lodge of England.

How strong is Orangeism globally?

The Grand Orange Lodge of Ireland is seen as the Premier Grand Lodge. There are also Grand Lodges in England, Scotland, USA, Canada, New Zealand, Australia, Togo and Ghana. The Imperial Orange Council is the all-embracing group overseeing Orangeism around the world and it meets every three years.

In Togo there are fewer than a hundred Orangemen, mainly attached to two churches. They are very evangelical and involved in Christian outreach work; however, their social profile in that country is very high. The lodge members include surgeons, civil servants and businessmen. The Orange in Togo is an urban organisation based entirely in the capital. In Ghana it's a rural organisation based largely around churches in the country areas.

How do they differ from Orangemen here?

Obviously they're different in that they are African. But in the sense of being interested in Christian fellowship and outreach work and belonging to a fraternity, there are tremendous similarities. Orange lodges in Ghana are quite popular. There are about a thousand members in Ghana. Masonic lodges in Ghana are very, very strong, to the extent that when the Grand Masonic Lodge meets, it's reported in the daily papers. During the coup in Ghana, when Rawlings was in power, Masonic lodge meetings were banned. It was feared these meetings could be used as cover to plot against the coup. Orange lodge meetings were also banned. So they had to meet informally for several years. This was Orange history repeating itself, albeit in a country far removed from nineteenth-century Ireland. The ban in Ghana has recently been lifted.

Credit unions in Northern Ireland were set up by John Hume, the Nobel Peace Prize winner and former leader of the SDLP, and as such were perceived by most Protestants to be a 'Catholic thing'. How did Orangemen get involved in organising credit unions?

The Orange Order has two pillars within it. One is the Protestant religion and the other is a fraternal mutual support organisation. Two years ago we had an internal membership survey done by an English university. Orangemen were asked what were the most important aspects of the Order for them personally and those two pillars of religion and fraternity scored quite highly, which is an indication that many members understand what the Order is about.

Credit unions are mutual support organisations. They fit in perfectly with the ethos of the Order. So it was not a surprise to me that within the Protestant community the unions were promoted and facilitated by Orange lodges. Almost all the credit unions in Protestant areas were instigated by members of the Order and almost all of them have their offices in Orange Halls. Within the unionist community, it wasn't the churches that started up the credit unions, it wasn't the great and the good, it wasn't the voluntary action groups or the Women's Institute, it was the Orange Order. We've demonstrated we can take the lead in terms of community development amongst our own people in actually doing that.

The lesson to be learnt from the history of credit unions in Ireland is that the Protestant community is approximately thirty years behind the Catholic community in terms of organisation and at least twenty years behind in terms of community activity. There has to be some reason why we are so far behind. A hundred years ago, Protestants in Ireland were very well organised and very active. In the late 1890s the Order campaigned for the building of its own premises and that resulted in over seven hundred halls being constructed over the next decade. In those days, that was a fantastic effort by any community-based group. Later there was resistance to Home Rule which led to the formation of an army, and the Protestant people were so well organised that we were able to carve out our own state. If you were to ask is the Protestant community as well organised today, the answer would patently be no!

So what happened between the early part of the twentieth century and the late part of the twentieth century that robbed Protestants of the ability to organise for themselves. My theory is that it was all down to Stormont. For fifty years we had 'Big Daddy' Stormont and it did everything for unionists and, as a community, Protestants lost the ability to do things for themselves. In the early 1970s, after the fall of Stormont, there were years in the wilderness and years of confusion. It is only now, thirty years later that we are starting to regain the ability as a community to do things for ourselves.

Where was the Orange Order at that time? Why did it not offer the leadership to the Protestant people who you say had lost their way?

Our energies were diverted for thirty years by security considerations. At the start of the Troubles and throughout the years of terrorist violence, we encouraged our members to join the security forces. In the late 1980s, we saw a campaign of attacks on Orange halls and parades. The Order had 311 Orangemen murdered during the Troubles and more than two hundred of those were serving with the security forces. That represents an incredible sacrifice for any organisation in Northern Ireland. During the conflict, the most active members of the Orange Order, including myself and many other senior members, found all their energies diverted into serving as part-time members of the security forces – be it as Reserve police officers or as soldiers in the Ulster Defence Regiment. That is why we didn't get involved in community development work, that's why we didn't seek out grants to fix up our Orange Halls, that's why we didn't run recruitment campaigns for those thirty years.

When did all that change?

It changed for me when the UDR was disbanded, but I think I am on the cusp of the change in terms of my age group [late forties]. People older than me have a different attitude. If something happens, they write to their MP about it or write to Grand Lodge about it; they basically try to get someone else to do something about it rather than doing something about it themselves. People who are younger than me adopt the attitude – what are WE going to do about it, WE must do something ourselves rather than leave it to others.

So the change within the Protestant community came

about gradually, as people of my age and younger came into positions of seniority and power within different organisations. If you were to take a look at all the people now involved in community development work in the unionist community, the vast majority of them will all be aged under fifty.

Are Orange halls off limits to Catholics?

Not at all. Credit unions based in Orange halls have Catholic members. In some areas, the percentage of Protestant/Catholic membership mirrors that of the population of the town where the credit union is based. It is a fallacy to say all Orange halls are off limits to Catholics. There might be one or two exceptions, but you'd be hard pressed to find an Orange hall that has a rule that states 'No Catholics' across the door.

Does the Orange Order have an association with loyalist paramilitaries?

No, we have no association with loyalist paramilitaries. We disapprove of what they've done in the past and what they seem to continue to do. We think that they should stand down. Our attitude is that paramilitary activity is incompatible with membership of the Orange Order. We also understand that occasionally we will have had members who were involved with the paramilitaries. But we also have members who are not involved with paramilitaries, members who are clergymen, politicians etc.

Does the Order come down hard enough on those members who breach the

rules and are suspected of being paramilitaries?

If someone is caught and convicted of paramilitary activity, we would expect that person to resign from the Order. Secondly if they didn't resign, the Order would expect that person's lodge to take disciplinary proceedings to suspend or expel them.

Would expulsion not be the least an Orangeman should expect if convicted of such an offence?

Unfortunately disciplinary powers do not reside at the top at Grand Lodge level. We are a very democratic organisation. These powers start at local lodge level. We, at Grand Lodge level, are also mature enough to accept that discipline is not enforced as much as it should be in some instances. Again, we are a vast organisation and we do our best to encourage lodges to enforce discipline uniformly across the province but we know it doesn't always happen. I accept that where that occurs and disciplinary procedures are not enforced against certain individuals, it creates a certain image.

Northern Ireland is a very morally ambivalent society, in particular in the political life of the province. We see paramilitary leaders, loyalist and republican, being treated as statesmen by our own government. We see them being financed by our own government in terms of schemes for members of terrorist organisations. We see senior members of the IRA who have been responsible for many murders, including the murders of Orangemen, being treated by the government as ordinary citizens. We

225

see our Secretary of State, Peter Hain, being among a group of English MPs who sent fraternal greetings to a Sinn Féin conference a number of years ago. All of these things have created this moral ambivalence which we as a Loyal Order and all of society in Northern Ireland have been partially sucked into.

Do two wrongs make a right?

No, they do not. While we encourage our lodges to do the right thing at all times, we know that because of this ambivalence in our society, some of them will take a different view. Disciplinary action must start at local lodge level. They have to initiate the disciplinary action, except against members of Grand Lodge where the Grand Master can initiate the action. Under the current structures of the Order, Grand Lodge cannot step in and involve itself in initiating an action at local lodge level where no Grand Lodge member is involved. It would involve a change in our rules, which I feel may come.

Obviously we are trying to address the discipline issue and we are looking at the rules. As it stands, the Grand Master is not empowered to enforce discipline against ordinary members of the institution, although he is empowered to enforce discipline in certain very limited circumstances against the approximately 150 members of Grand Lodge.

Personally speaking, I think the rules should change. There have been suggestions that conviction for certain offences or being sentenced to a period of imprisonment should lead to automatic expulsion from the Order. We have discussed this and it's likely that the rule change will come in. It is a live issue at the moment, but funnily enough as Northern Ireland becomes a more peaceful society, this issue is going to become less live. Over the next decade I think lodge members convicted of sex offences are more likely to be a problem for the Orange Order than paramilitary connections. That issue is also under consideration and it's likely that any Orangeman placed on the Sex Offenders Register will face automatic expulsion.

We also have to bear in mind that we have members who have gone to prison in the past for non-payment of fines because they took part in protests, in particular against the Public Processions Order which targeted Orange parades. Some people took a stand against that on a point of principle. They were convicted, they refused to pay their fines and went to jail over it. So obviously people like that are not going to be expelled.

How much of a problem is it to be associated with flute bands that have close ties to loyalist paramilitaries and to have leading loyalists claim that the Orange Order has used their muscle to clear a particular road for lodges to march down?

Regarding the bands, it is illegal for them to carry anything that implies support for an illegal paramilitary organisation. I hear what you are saying but I think it's out of date. There certainly should not be any band involved in an Orange parade carrying anything that implies support for the present-day UVF, which is an illegal organisation, or the UDA. In truth, I was a little bit surprised when I made enquiries about this and I was told that the bands have stopped doing this. So, my understanding is that they no longer carry anything implying support for illegal groups. Some bands do carry standards or flags which refer to the historic UVF from the Battle of Somme in the 1914–18 World War. That's quite legitimate and that's a part of our history. We're proud of that and I have no difficulty with it. We would not engage a band that carries any insignia or flags that imply support for an illegal organisation.

As regards the claims that we use loyalist muscle – we would not do that. Local loyalist communities, including some paramilitaries, have been involved in marshalling at Orange parades but they are doing in it such a way as to be a restraining influence on the Protestants of that community. They are not marshalling the Orangemen on parade, because we have our own marshals within the local lodges. We actually send our own people to night colleges to be trained in marshalling techniques. While we have lots of volunteers, we've had trouble securing the funding for it, because in some areas the local authorities tell us there is no bother with Orange parades and therefore it's not necessary to fund the training of marshals.

There have been a number of incidents during Orange marches when those on parade have been guilty of incitement. How does the Order intend to maintain discipline and dignity amongst those on parade?

The chap who put the five fingers up during an Orange

parade [as it passed a bookie's shop where five Catholics were murdered by loyalist gunmen] *was more or less disciplined on the spot. I think he was suspended from the Order that night. Being provocative by playing Orange music outside Catholic churches should not happen. We are totally against that and if a band does do that, we tell them to stop doing it.*

In 2006, the Orange Institution for the first time organised what it called an 'Orange Fest in Belfast'. What's that about?

For about five or six years now, people have been talking about trying to make Twelfth of July Orange demonstrations more like a festival. That has led to study trips and an official Orange delegation going to the Notting Hill Carnival in London in 2004. The delegation met the organisers, local councillors and the police who explained how that event was carried off. In 2005, our delegation visited an area in the Basque region of Spain to watch a disputed parade. In September of each year in Hondarribia, they have a parade called the 'Alarde', celebrating the relief of the walled city from siege in the 1630s. It bears a striking resemblance to the Apprentice Boys of Derry parades in Londonderry commemorating the relief of that city in the 1680s.

[The Apprentice Boys of Derry are a separate loyal Protestant order. The Apprentice Boys have no direct link to the Orange Institution other than the fact that some of its members are also Orangemen. The Apprentice Boys organisation takes its name from the thirteen young apprentices who, during the siege of Derry in 1688, closed the gates of the city in the face of the enemy forces loyal to Catholic King James. Despite being besieged, the city held out and played a critical role in the eventual victory of the Williamite forces in Europe during what became known as the Glorious Revolution.]

The Alarde parade is contentious, with police in riot gear out in force along the route. Despite this, it still takes place annually and is advertised in the local tourist literature. It was rather ironic that our delegation was there watching this parade in Spain at the same time as the Whiterock Orange parade, and all the trouble surrounding it, was taking place in Belfast. We met everybody involved with the Spanish event and we learnt lessons there, including the importance of civic involvement.

Traditionally Orange parades here are organised by the local lodges with no civic involvement whatever. Life has become more complicated now in terms of public health legislation and public safety measures, so you really need civic involvement to create an atmosphere where everyone can feel comfortable. That was our first big lesson learned.

How will those lessons play out on the ground at Orange parades in Northern Ireland?

There are up to fifteen annual Twelfth of July Orange demonstrations in Northern Ireland and we are encouraging people to make it more festival-like in the future.

This would mean the Twelfth would last longer and have a wider range of attractions. Typically it would be a week of events of which the Twelfth Orange parade is just one of the attractions and probably the culmination of the festival. It would also involve outreach events such as historic talks for the general public including those from the nationalist community.

Is it necessary for the Orange Institution to be a marching Order?
Armies march, we parade and it is necessary for us to parade. That is why young men join the Orange Order. They want to do something to show their Britishness. They want to say, 'I'm proud of my heritage and my background. I am proud to be an Ulster Protestant and I want to display that visibly.' In my opinion, that is the main reason why a lot of young men join the Orange. Parading is such an integral part of our culture and I could not envisage that changing in my lifetime. However, we do encourage people to seek out other ways of displaying their Britishness.

Is it probable that in future there will be fewer Orange parades each year?
In my opinion, looking at it logically, there probably would be fewer parades as time goes on. In reality, however, the opposite appears to be happening. I think there are more parades because Orange activists are appearing in different areas and they want to have their own wee parade. The traditional parades never tend to die out even if the numbers go down. So the older parades still

happen and new ones come along from time to time that add to the total number. I can see the nature of our parades changing and I would encourage that. I would encourage the parades to change from being demonstrations that have political overtones into being cultural festivals. Hopefully those changes and other things that we're doing at a higher level within the institution, in terms of cross-community contact, will create a better atmosphere that will be able to resolve at least some of the contentious parades issues.

Something appears to be changing within Orangeism. What is it?

We are coming out of the Troubles and now we are able to divert more of our time, thoughts and energy into planning for the future, rather just reacting to the attacks on our institution that we've had for thirty years. We are starting to be more outward looking rather than inward looking.

In recent months, the Order has been involved in a number of groundbreaking meetings with the Irish government, the SDLP and the leader of the Catholic Church in Ireland. Did this cause one or two Orangemen to drop their teacups in Orange halls around the country?

One or two, yes; however, the reaction has been very supportive. Obviously we record the number of phone calls to Orange HQ when issues like this arise. During the Spirit of Drumcree protests we had dozens of calls of complaint every day from Orangemen. We had only one call of complaint over our recent series of meetings. I think there is a maturity of debate within the institution's membership that wasn't there a few years ago. People are thinking about it a bit more. The days of the knee-jerk reaction are gone. Our people are realising that street protests did not achieve the aim, so now we are trying a different tactic. However, I don't want people to think that meeting the Catholic Church hierarchy and the SDLP was a tactic. These were genuine meetings. Our aim initially has been to convince them of our bona fides. We want to sort out the parades issue. We want to do it in a mature way and we want to do it while consulting with them. These contacts are good because we were able to make points to them about how worrying we find it that 50 per cent of their community votes for people who have been involved in, or are associated with, those involved in a murder campaign. We pointed out to them that the Protestant community has never done that. Generally speaking when it comes to politics, paramilitary-associated candidates in the Protestant community won't get elected. We find it baffling and certainly worrying that such a large percentage of the Roman Catholic community will vote for people like that. Clearly there is a different level of tolerance of violence within the two communities.

Is the Order still convinced that the parades problem was brought about as part of a plot by Sinn Féin?

Yes, we are. In the first twenty years of the Troubles, there was no real opposition to parades and there were only four Orange halls set on fire. Since 1989, there have been 242 halls burnt. It was around that time that the

Republican movement started to oppose our parades in the Tunnel area and Obins Street in Portadown and then the Garvaghy Road. This spread to other parts of Northern Ireland. Republicans started attacking the Order by burning Orange halls and opposing parades. There are two possible analyses of this strategy. Firstly, the Republican leadership was involved in secret contacts with the British government at this time and they wanted to wean their foot-soldiers off bombings and attacks on the security forces, on to different targets. The second is that Sinn Féin had to prove to the British government that the 'Orange card' was a fallacy and that if the British government pulled out of Northern Ireland, Orangemen and Protestants would not rise up and massacre the Catholic population. They had to show that attacks on us would not lead to Protestants taking up guns en masse against the Catholic population. [Drew Nelson draws a distinction between this scenario and the violence surrounding the Drumcree protests. He says that was street violence and not on a par with gun violence.]

The Public Processions Northern Ireland Act came into force, which was essentially a political concession to nationalists. It created the Parades Commission and that has made the parades situation worse and it is getting less and less tolerable for us. The nature of the legislation and the work of the Parades Commission mean that more and more parades are becoming contentious. The Commission has created a 'charter for protestors', who can cause a lot of trouble for the Order's parades with very little cost to themselves. In my opinion, people who just want to create trouble are going to climb on the bandwagon. I'm concerned the parading issue is going to get bigger over the next few years. There are fewer problems with the handful of really contentious parades, but more and more local parades are coming into the contentious bracket. This is leading to restrictions being placed on them, which is driving Orangemen up the walls.

Increasingly it is becoming a big issue for our community. It comes up every year and people are getting very hot under the 'collarette' about it. On 14 July 2005, we set up a Joint Loyal Orders Working Group to address these issues, and this is the group that's been involved in meeting a range of people. We are engaged in an initiative to persuade the government to review the parades legislation. [The JLOWG comprises the Orange, the Black, and the Independent Orange, but not the Apprentice Boys.]

The Orange Order doesn't want the parades decision-making process to revert to the police again, so what does it hope to get out of a review?
We don't want a free-for-all and the right to parade everywhere. We understand that someone has to take the decision on parades if there is a dispute about them. The difficulty is that the legislation that established the Parades Commission is partial. It gives the nationalist community a veto over expressions of Protestant culture. We want new legislation, we believe that is essential.

How did you feel when two members of the Orange Order recently joined

the Parades Commission?

I was amazed. Our policy within the Order is to have no contact with the Commission. We regard it as part of the problem, not part of the solution, and we don't want to give it credibility. However, the fact that they had to resign their membership of the Order to take up their posts shows how one-sided it is. You can have senior GAA and SDLP people sitting on the Commission without having to resign those positions. Yet they can sit in judgment on our parades.

How was the Orange Order affected by the conflict in Northern Ireland?

Almost all of the 311 Orangemen murdered during the Troubles were killed by the Provisional IRA. For most of those killed, a photograph of the victim will hang in the lodge room to remind the other members of the sacrifice that has been made. Those murders have left an unresolved issue of resentment amongst the Orange Institution and it exhibits itself in one of two ways. The first is great anger at how we've been treated by the PSNI, where police officers must declare Orange Order membership like a notifiable disease. For an organisation which has encouraged its members to serve in the police throughout the years of the Troubles – which led to so many of them being killed – we find that very, very hard to take and very demeaning. That has created a real anger within the institution and, in my opinion, it is alienating people from the organs of the state. We hold both the government and the PSNI responsible for that.

The second thing is this: at the same time as the Orange Order is being demonised within the PSNI, we see new recruits being encouraged and allowed to wear IRA medals won by their grandparents. [Since January 2006 decorations and medals awarded by a foreign state or any society may be worn by a member of the PSNI on whom they have been conferred, if authorised by the Chief Constable.] *We see the PSNI GAA team being encouraged, with senior officers attending their matches as a sign of encouragement. So it seems to us that within the PSNI there is a partisan favouritism towards the Catholic community, at our expense.*

What would you see as a way of redressing that supposed 'imbalance'?
The first thing they should do is remove the necessity for PSNI members to declare membership of the Orange Order. Secondly, the police should do something that would be a clear sign to us that they are going to treat both communities fairly. We are not against the police having a GAA team; it's the way that it is clearly favoured by the powers-that-be, with senior officers right up to Chief Constable attending their matches.

Was there ever an Orange lodge within the RUC?
No, not within the police. There have been Orange lodges that had an internal lodge rule stating that you had to be a serving or ex-member of the RUC before you could join. I wouldn't want to see an Orange lodge within the police. I don't think that's the proper thing to do either. We want

the PSNI to show us that we are wanted. Are we a valued section of the community to them or are we not? And the signals we're getting at the minute are that we are not. The Chief Constable, Sir Hugh Orde, gave a major interview recently to a Belfast newspaper in which he gave a warning specifically to the Orange Order, indicating that if people break parades determinations, he would come after us. He doesn't seem to be going after other people involved in contentious parades.

Criticism of the Order and its leadership has come from inside and outside the institution in recent years. Do you feel it was valid criticism?

I think almost none of it is warranted. Brian Kennaway's book – and I've only read excerpts from it – is, in my opinion, about personal grievances going back a number of years. I understand the general thrust of his criticism that we're not outgoing enough in meeting the nationalist community and the Catholic Church. Essentially those criticisms are history now because we have gone past that.

In times of crisis, Orange leaders have managed to put their 'foot in their mouth' with alarming regularity. How do you ensure that you don't repeat those public faux pas?

We have had some public relations disasters in the past. In a sense, we are an organisation that is not very well equipped to deal with these things. In the future, we intend to modernise; we are going to change and we are going to be much better prepared for things like that. The people who were involved in those PR disasters were not experienced in dealing with the press and they were thrown into situations not all of their own making. I have sympathy for them because they just were not equipped to deal with the problems they were faced with. It's almost a sign of the innocence of the Orange Order in these matters although it's maybe better to put it down to lack of experience.

When the Order is clearly in the wrong, would it not be better to admit it rather than try to lay the blame elsewhere?

Yes, that would be my attitude. However, it may not be other people's attitude. Mistakes have happened; if we make mistakes, we should admit them, learn from them and try not to repeat them.

Where will the Orange Order be in ten years' time?

I think in another ten years it will be more influential within the Protestant community. We have been almost without influence for decades and that may come as a surprise to some people. Our views have been ignored, but I think that because of increasing activity at grassroots level, and increasing community involvement, we will actually become more influential within society in the next decade. An organisation like the Orange that stands for upholding the law, for encouraging church attendance and responsible citizenship has got to be a good thing for society. We call it 'local lodges, local leaders'. One of our strategic aims is to develop leadership at this level and to encourage people to become leaders in all aspects of their community. That includes in their churches, it includes forming credit unions, it includes local community groups, rural development groups, and it even includes becoming involved in politics. While we would like to see Orange parades developing into an enjoyable day for everyone, much more work will be done in the background supporting our own local communities. In the 1960s, Orange lodges were involved in parades, social functions and, to a certain extent, politics, and I think that in future the level of community activity is going to increase vastly.

The number of professionally qualified people who are active within the institution will increase. There are almost no people in my own profession (law) who are older than me and who are active within the Orange Order. In terms of my age group and lower, there are quite a number. I would accept that in the past we probably had more professional people as members but they often were not active within the Order. In the future, we are going to have more of those professionally qualified members getting actively involved in the institution.

The big test for us is to stay relevant within society. In very broad terms, our relevance, from 1886 onwards, was our resistance to Home Rule in Ireland. From 1921 onwards, it was to support the administration at Stormont. When the Troubles started in the late 1960s early 1970s, our relevance was as protectors of the community through involvement in the part-time security forces. However, our relevance as a social organisation declined throughout the Troubles because people stopped going to dances and functions in Orange Halls.

The question is: what will make us relevant for the next generation? In my opinion, that will be the religious and fraternal aspects of Orangeism, worked out through community involvement. I see us providing ground-level leadership in hundreds of small towns and villages throughout Northern Ireland. We already have up to seventy Credit Unions operating in Orange halls and we have encouraged and are leading hundreds of community groups who are also meeting in our halls. That's what's keeping us relevant.

CHAPTER 8

THE INDEPENDENT
LOYAL ORANGE
INSTITUTION

There is a popular misconception that the Independent Loyal Orange Institution is the creation of its most prominent member, DUP leader Ian Paisley. In fact, it is more than a hundred years old and at its core are the religious and political divisions of the opening years of the twentieth century. The Independent Orange's motto is 'Protestantism not politics, principles not party and measures not men.'

The organisation has about a thousand members drawn mainly from the North and Mid-Ulster areas and it is more radical, Presbyterian and working class.

In the booklet *A chosen few*, which outlines the history and impact of the Independent Institution, Imperial Grand Master George Dawson states,

> We are unionists, but our unionism is as a result of our Protestantism. Protestantism is international, it is a body of doctrine which cannot be confined by borders or politics.

However, it remains our simple belief that freedom to practise our Protestant religion is better protected within a United Kingdom than in a United Ireland.

This fracturing from the Orange family was precipitated by politics but at the heart of the matter was a growing religious rent. The rift came about after an incident during Twelfth of July proceedings at the Belfast County demonstration in Castlereagh in the east of the city in 1902. The mood was black even before the guest speakers took to the platform to address the Orangemen. Trouble had been fermenting amongst the rank-and-file members who were concerned that their Order was being infiltrated by men with 'selfish and political interests'. Earlier that same year, an Orange parade in Rostrevor in South Down had been banned by the Conservative and Unionist government. Word filtered out that some Orange Order leaders had been consulted ahead of the decision and given it their approval.

At the Belfast Twelfth parade to Orangefield in Castlereagh, Orangeman Tom Sloan, who was Worshipful Master of St Michael's Total Abstinence Lodge and a leading member of the Belfast Protestant Association, posed a question to the most senior Orangeman in the city. In front of the assembled brethren he confronted the County Grand Master, Colonel Saunderson, who was also the local Conservative and Unionist Member of Parliament, asking him if he had voted against the inspection of the convent laundries which were suspected of abusing the young Catholic girls who worked in them.

Colonel Saunderson is reported to have replied,

'Certainly not', to which Sloan responded,

'Then the *Belfast Press* must be liars!'

The intervention achieved two things. From Sloan's perspective, it exposed a senior Orangeman 'going soft' on Catholics. There was a suspicion that Saunderson had come under the influence of the more liberal English Conservative MPs. Secondly, Sloan, a working man through and through, was effectively thumbing his nose at the political elite and the unionist ascendancy.

Thomas Henry Sloan was well known for his activities on behalf of the Belfast Protestant Association. He was also a member of the National Amalgamated Union of Labour, working as a plater in Belfast shipyard where he held regular evangelical meetings during his dinner hour. Descriptions of him range from a reluctant rebel and a sectarian bigot to a working-class hero and a forerunner of Edward Carson, the iconic Ulster Unionist leader at the time of partition.

Tom Sloan's stock rose following his stand and, bolstered by the support of many brethren, he won a Westminster seat in the South Belfast by-election, but the confrontation in the field came back to haunt him, ultimately damaging his fledgling political career.

Sloan was summoned to a meeting of the County Grand Lodge of Belfast, charged with conduct unbecoming to an Orangeman, during the platform proceedings on 12 July. He was eventually accused of insulting the County Grand Master with his remarks about the convent laundries. When Sloan appeared before his accusers, he was armed with a copy of Hansard containing the official verbatim report of parliamentary proceedings which, he claimed, proved the point he had made on the speakers' platform in Castlereagh. It was a futile gesture. Sloan was suspended from the Orange Order for two years. The County lodge also withdrew the warrants of three private Orange lodges, and several individual brethren who had supported Sloan were suspended from the Order. Sloan appealed his suspension to the Grand Lodge of Ireland, but to no avail. The County and Grand Lodge proceedings led him and his supporters to believe that the Conservatives and Unionists within the Orange Order had cracked the whip to bring about his downfall.

If the Orange Grandees thought that they had seen off the challenge of the socialist upstart from Belfast shipyard, they were in for a shock. The following year, on 11 June 1903, many of the suspended Orangemen and their supporters gathered in an area that is now home to the Belfast Botanical Gardens. It was agreed to form an Independent Loyal Orange Institution, bringing about the most serious schism in the Order since its foundation. A month later, crowds, reported at more than two thousand people, attended the new Independent Order's first public demonstration at Knock in East Belfast, predictably on the Twelfth of July.

Within months, Orange warrants were being returned in support of the Independents; these included Ballymoney District Lodge, Rasharkin, Ballycastle and Portglenone. When the Independent Loyal Orange Institution held its second Twelfth of July celebration in what was now its bedrock area of County Antrim and mid-Ulster, more than thirty lodges and bands took part in the parade. In Belfast, twenty-five lodges joined the breakaway Order, along with six in North Armagh and South

Down. Many lodges were designated either Temperance or Abstinence – in reality, teetotal. That became a general rule of the institution in 1904 and remains so to this day.

The Independent Order's leader, Tom Sloan, came under the influence of Lindsay Crawford, an evangelical Protestant from Lisburn. Crawford, a member of the Church of Ireland, was vociferous in his opposition to Anglican Church ritualism and Roman Catholicism. He was a journalist by profession and at that time was editor of the *Irish Protestant*, which was published in Dublin. Although Sloan is acknowledged as a founding father of the Independent Orange Order, Crawford was elected its first Grand Master at the inaugural meeting of the Independent Imperial Grand Orange Lodge in February 1904. It is thought that Crawford was selected ahead of Sloan because of his previous experience as a member of the Grand Orange Lodge of Ireland.

Historian Dr Eamon Phoenix says that Crawford brought a radical notion to the breakaway Orange movement. 'He was obviously an intellectual and he was the philosopher of the new Independent Orange movement,' he says, pointing out that Crawford was also the architect of the Magheramourne Manifesto, introduced at an Independent Orange Twelfth demonstration in Magheramourne near Larne in County Antrim on 13 July 1905. The manifesto called for a fraternity of Irishmen and condemned rule from Dublin Castle. According to Phoenix, it also seemed to point in the direction of Home Rule, 'making it a very, very radical document given its Orange source'.

There are many descriptions of Crawford and what he was trying to achieve with his Magheramourne manifesto. George

Dawson, who is the current Imperial Grand Master of the Independent Orange Order, believes that the Lisburn man had a vision of a strong, strident and organised Protestant movement, confident enough to persuade Irish nationalists that it would be in their best interests to embrace the principles of the Williamite Revolution Settlement, thus cementing the position of Ireland within the United Kingdom.

'He sought to persuade nationalists to become Orangemen and the result was that the Orangeman became a nationalist,' says Mr Dawson.

Tom Sloan was not converted to Crawford's ideas and, within a few years, the Independent Order had expelled its leading philosopher and first Grand Master.

Lindsay Crawford is the only prominent example of an evangelical Protestant who moves all the way from unionism and Orangeism to Irish republicanism. He eventually went to live in Canada where he became the editor of a Toronto newspaper and then, in 1922, he was appointed as the Irish Free State's Trade Representative in Washington.

MISSION STATEMENT

Today the Independent Order continues to promote the concept of Orangeism free from outside interference, dealing solely with the principles of Protestantism. It states categorically that it recognises the diversity of modern society, 'while maintaining our Independence from outside influence. We deny to no one the rights we expect for ourselves'.

If the Loyal Orange Institution of Ireland is a broad church organisation, the Independent Order is a parochial hall.

Historically those within the Independent Order viewed the Loyal Orange Order as being overtaken by class divisions, a political party and the Anglican Church. Before the split came about, there was a growing number of Presbyterians joining the Orange Order and that particular Protestant denomination was in the ascendancy following the disestablishment of the Church of Ireland in 1869. The working classes were sniffing at the winds of change blowing through rural Ireland and detecting the whiff of proletariate democracy in the air.

The Independent Order was as much Presbyterian as the Loyal Orange Order was Anglican at that time. Presbyterians see themselves as strongly democratic in everything they do. In their view, the Orange Order and its structures were anything but. Something had to give and eventually it did.

The Independent Order is against ecumenism and evangelism that embraces the Catholic Church. It states:

> We unapologetically declare our unchanging attachment to the historic evangelical Protestant faith. We stand with the reformers in declaring the Bible alone, grace alone, faith alone and Christ alone as the tenets of our faith. Consequently we reject Romanism, ritualism, sacramentalism, Unitarianism and ecumenism. Ecumenical contact with the Church of Rome is contrary to the word of God, subversive to the Gospel of free grace and detrimental to the well being of the state.

In uncompromisingly straightforward terms it declares the Roman Catholic doctrinal system to be widely divergent from the scriptures and evangelical beliefs, and points up the differences in Catholic Church worship and prayer:

> We cannot hope to see our Roman Catholic neighbours won for Christ, if it appears that we are condoning the religious system in which they are currently entrapped.

The Independent Order says that its members should encourage what it calls 'born again' Catholics to seek evangelical fellowship in a church 'where the Gospel of free grace is preached', and continues:

> To pray with Roman Catholics is to recognise their church's claim to be a true Christian denomination. This will simply compromise our evangelical faith, for the Roman Catholic church will not change.

STRUCTURES

The structure of the Independent Orange Order is much the same as that of the group from which it split over a hundred years earlier. Private lodges annually elect their office bearers. The Worshipful Master is the most senior officer in the lodge who, as chairman, conducts the business of the lodge meetings. He is assisted by a Deputy Master; a Chaplain who conducts the prayers and doctrinal matters; a Secretary who keeps the minutes and deals with the correspondence and reports; a Treasurer who keeps tabs on the money; the Lodge Committee men who make detailed arrangements for events and deputise for the senior officers; the Tylers who are the doormen and are responsible for making sure that only members of the Order are admitted to meetings.

Private lodges send representatives to their District lodge. The Districts then select representatives to attend the County Grand Lodge meetings and the County Grand Lodge makes up the most senior level in the Order – the Imperial Grand Lodge. A number of committees report to the Imperial Grand Lodge and they oversee the entire Independent Loyal Orange Institution in Northern Ireland, England, Scotland, Australia and anywhere else that an Independent Lodge exists.

LODGE WORKING AND DEGREES

The Independent Lodge operates similarly to the Loyal Order Lodge. Meetings are private and open only to members. This is ensured by a series of passwords, secret handshakes and special knocks. This information is imparted to new members by word of mouth through lectures and instruction.

The degree levels within the Independent Order are also similar to those in the Loyal Order. There are three – the Orange Degree, the Plain Purple Degree and the Royal Arch Purple Degree. The degrees represent levels of attainment through Bible instruction within the Order and reflect seniority. There is usually a six-month waiting period between each degree to allow time for reflection by both the candidate and the lodge before proceeding further within the institution. Those who press on to the Royal Arch Purple degree usually form the grandees of any lodge and are selected for important decision-making bodies within the institution.

The degrees themselves are based on biblical text. They are not written on paper, but are supposed to be memorised and passed on only through lectures and verbal instruction. The Order says that this experience fosters camaraderie and brotherhood amongst the brethren. The organisation defends its degree structure which from time to time has been attacked because of 'origins, symbols and content'. The Independent Order's robust response to this criticism is that the claims are 'poorly researched, unreliable, untruthful and based on questionable logic'.

PARADES

The Independent Order regards itself as non-party political although it acknowledges that all of its members are of a unionist viewpoint. The Independent Order is in full accordance with the Loyal Orange Order on the issue of parades and particularly the role of the Parades Commission.

The Independent Orange believes that by placing restrictions on Loyal Order parades, the Commission is 'reaching deep into the psyche of many individuals and inflicting a grievous hurt'. According to the Independent Order, parades are an integral part of the institution and always involve members walking to a religious service in a church or at an open-air gathering. When the lodges are marching, they are actually 'in session', meaning that the parade begins when the lodge meeting 'opens' in the Orange Hall and the meeting 'closes' only when the brethren return to the hall after the parade is over.

The Independents say that not being able to express public witness to their religious beliefs has left some of them feeling bereaved, angry, frustrated and isolated.

In a speech in July 2000, the Imperial Grand Master, George Dawson, outlined the Independent Order's position on Sinn Féin in government at Stormont:

> All it takes for evil to triumph is for good men to do nothing. Evil triumphed this week at the Northern Ireland Assembly when prominent Orangemen abstained in the vote to exclude Sinn Féin/IRA from government. Their action makes the infamous Colonel Lundy of the Siege of Londonderry appear a hero by comparison. Orangemen in the Ulster Unionist Assembly team who failed to vote for the exclusion ... should be removed from platforms and consigned to the wilderness of infamy.

Three years later, during the Independent Institution's centenary celebrations, the leadership took stock of the current situation in Northern Ireland. A banquet to mark the one hundredth birthday was held in Coleraine in County Antrim, and among the guests was the Grand Master of the Grand Lodge of Ireland, Robert Saulters. This was a significant moment and marked a turning point in the sometimes frosty relations that had existed between the two Orders. A century earlier, members from both Orders had been involved in pitched battles and fist fights in the street over their differences. The key that unlocked the door between the Independent Order and its predecessor was the breaking of the link between the Grand Orange Lodge of Ireland and the Ulster Unionist Party.

'Relations between the two Orange Orders have never been

better,' says George Dawson, the Imperial Grand Master of the Independent Order. 'Even members of the Royal Black Institution have attended some of our events recently.'

Dawson is a member of the Democratic Unionist Party and an elected representative to the Stormont Assembly. His party leader, Dr Ian Paisley, is probably the best-known Orangeman within the Independent Order, along with his DUP colleague and fellow Assembly Member Gregory Campbell from Londonderry.

George Dawson has been a prominent member of the Joint Loyal Orders' Working Group, involved in a series of groundbreaking meetings with nationalist politicians and the head of the Catholic Church in Ireland, Archbishop Seán Brady.

'This coming togetherness is good for the Loyal Orders,' says George Dawson. 'On core issues like parades and Protestantism, we can cooperate and will continue to cooperate while retaining our separate identities.'

Dawson was also a member of the Democratic Unionist Party's negotiation team which attended the St Andrews talks in Scotland in October 2006. All the main political parties from Northern Ireland took part in the discussions to try to find a way of breaking the deadlock over restoring a devolved power-sharing administration at Stormont. The two main players in this constitutional high-stakes game were the DUP and Sinn Féin.

Taken individually, these incidents of dialogue are important enough, but viewed in the round they have an even greater significance; just a few years ago, the idea of a Joint Loyal Orders Working Group meeting such a range of people on the cusp of another 'marching season' was practically unthinkable.

Whether the meetings of the group are judged to be historic rests with the historians and the passage of time, but they represent a significant departure from what was the 'norm' in matters concerning the Loyal Orders in Northern Ireland for as long as anyone can remember.

CHAPTER 9

A NEW BEGINNING

Policemen wearing riot helmets and wielding truncheons waded into groups of nationalist protestors. One young man stood up, his hands in the air in a passive gesture. The RUC officer drew back his baton and brought it crashing down on the man's head. He fell to the ground, unconscious, blood trickling from his wound onto the street as mayhem ensued on Belfast's Ormeau Bridge that day. Spanning the River Lagan in south Belfast, the bridge carries one of the main approach routes into the city centre. The protesters had been sitting down on the carriageway to prevent a Loyal Order parade from passing through the mainly Catholic Lower Ormeau Road. The RUC officers had been told by their commanders to clear the road and that meant physically lifting or dragging the people away. As the line of police officers moved forward, the protesters, some linking arms, huddled together. When the first blow was struck, there was pandemonium as men and women tried desperately to scramble clear of the trouble while others traded blows with police officers. It was just one of many disturbing scenes witnessed on the Ormeau Road in the late 1990s, including a hail of missiles raining down on the RUC lines from the loyalist side of the river and the astonishing sight of police officers in modern-day riot gear being attacked by a loyal order member wielding his ceremonial pike.

The TV news cameras relayed these images to a nationwide audience. The events brought home the brutality that was born out of the parading issue, and the blood from it flowed through the streets of those communities caught up in the crisis that gripped parts of Northern Ireland during the worst years of the contentious marching season.

When the trouble peaked in the mid- to late 1990s, the lower Ormeau Road was as much a tinderbox as Drumcree. Numerous Loyal Order demonstrations were banned from marching along the route on their way to the city centre, following opposition from the nationalist residents' group. On two occasions – 1999 and 2000 – the Orange Order 'rerouted' the city's annual Twelfth demonstration to nearby Ormeau Park in support of the local Ballynafeigh Orange lodges. This posed a major security headache for the police as thousands of Orangemen and bandsmen, along with their supporters, descended on the municipal park directly across the River Lagan from the nationalist houses in the Lower Ormeau. Large-scale security operations were put in place in the Ormeau Road area, with police and soldiers deployed along the route and a huge steel barrier erected across the Ormeau Bridge which spans the river. This was as far as the Ballynafeigh lodges got on their 'traditional' route to join the rest of the Belfast County lodges in the city centre. A familiar routine was established. When the marchers reached the security barrier, a letter of protest expressing anger at the re-routing would be handed over to a senior police officer. The lodge members and bandsmen would then hold a brief religious service or protest rally at the barrier, before dispersing or boarding buses that would take them to the city centre via another route. I reported on many of these contentious parades in the Ormeau area. Some passed off peacefully; others descended into violence.

Reporting live on BBC Radio Ulster during one of these parades along the Ormeau Road, I was interviewed on the telephone by the late Barry Cowan, who was presenting the news and current affairs programme of the day. Barry was a vastly experienced and highly respected presenter, who had seen it all before in a career spanning more than twenty years in broadcasting. I detected a note of exasperation in his voice when he asked me,

'Mervyn ... do see any change in the attitudes of people on the ground there regarding the parades stalemate?'

I cast my eyes around the assembled marchers and nationalist protesters and replied,

'Barry, the only thing changing up here is the traffic lights.'

SMALL STEPS

A walk along the Ormeau Road today is a more pleasant experience. New cafés and shops occupy what were once drab or disused spaces, business appears to be thriving and there is a confidence about the place and its people. The parades problem has not gone away, but it has faded like the protest murals and slogans painted on the gable walls.

As the rest of the world entered the new millennium, any

changes in the Northern Ireland parading situation were imperceptible. Behind the scenes, however, something was happening. The violent protests at the Drumcree stand-off subsided and then disappeared. The Lower Ormeau also dropped below the security radar. There were problems at other parading venues, such as Dunloy, Ardoyne and the Springfield Road; but through it all, serious discussions were taking place in the background. The Parades Commission was still *persona non grata* in the eyes of Grand Lodge, but contact had been established with nationalist residents' groups.

In Londonderry, where violence had also marked contentious marches during the 1990s, real progress had been made towards resolving the parades problem. In the 'maiden' city – unbreached by the army of Catholic King James in 1688–89 after the thirteen young apprentices slammed the gates in his face and the defenders shouted 'No surrender' from the city walls – the loyal Orders seemed to be streets ahead of their colleagues elsewhere in Northern Ireland.

The Apprentice Boys of Derry (ABOD) – a loyal Order established to commemorate the young men who closed the gates and the defenders of the city – has an estimated membership of ten thousand. It has no affiliations to Orangeism, other than the fact that some of its members are also Orangemen. Records show that the first ABOD club was formed in 1714, and since that time all initiations into the order are carried out at the Order's headquarters within the ancient walled city itself. The organisation is inextricably linked to Londonderry and this has been a major constituent during its negotiations over parades in the city. The Apprentice Boys, the other loyal Orders, the nationalist residents and the business community in Derry have all played important roles in the discussions. The former SDLP leader, Derry resident and Nobel peace-prize winner, John Hume, was also involved in the process.

The depth of experience around the talks table would have been considerable. All could cite examples of how one side had trampled over the rights of the other in the preceding decades. The civil rights issue has resounded around Derry's Walls for generations. In October 1968, the unionist-controlled Stormont government banned a Civil Rights march due to take place from Duke Street in the Waterside area of the city. This resulted in violent scenes being captured on television cameras; police officers, wielding batons, ran amok amongst the marchers, beating people to the ground, and water cannon were used for the first time as a public order dispersal tool. This incident was compounded beyond belief when just over three years later, in January 1972, the British army shot dead thirteen civilians during rioting after another banned Civil Rights demonstration in the city. Westminster, where consecutive British governments had more or less turned a blind eye to how Northern Ireland was being governed, was provoked into action. The growing public disorder problem led to mounting pressure at home and abroad, pushing Downing Street into a more direct involvement in the running of Northern Ireland; that involvement has continued to this day.

In this context, the reaching of compromise between orange and green in a city with such a bloody history is all the more remarkable as Neil Jarman of the Institute for Conflict Research explains: 'Realistically, Londonderry is the only place to publicly acknowledge that they've done a deal and got a positive outcome.'

A compromise on parades was reached to which the Orange, the Black and the Apprentice Boys all agreed.

'I think in Derry there is a strong sense of the city, a strong sense of place which influences the process, plus the cross-membership within the loyal Orders,' Jarman continues. 'If the Apprentice Boys of Derry have done a deal, then their members who are also in the Orange and Black are able to influence those other organisations. But generally speaking, if you look at somewhere like the Lower Ormeau Road which was as big a problem as Drumcree, it's been completely off the agenda in recent years.' People have learned to live with the new situation in the Lower Ormeau Road, which is that the parade has been rerouted. 'Like so many stalemate situations, people have arrived at a new form of accommodation,' Jarman says. 'The nationalists know the parade is not getting down and the Orange are living with the rerouting.'

Contact with the nationalist residents in Derry may have paid off for the local Loyal Orders in the city, but it was still criticised by more conservative members of the Orange Order. This sort of criticism, in the face of what many observers would describe as 'a result', exposes the levels of contrasting, and at times confusing, opinions within Orangeism on parading.

Historian Eamon Phoenix believes that there has been a level of disarray within Orangeism since the 1980s and he says that this was accelerated by the signing of the Belfast Agreement in 1998.

'I can see the institution separating into two groups,' he says.

'You have the liberal, churchgoing, bible-orientated section of the Order, many of whom are farmers and respectable businessmen, who were turned off by what happened during the worst years of the Drumcree dispute. Then you have this kind of lumping proletariat within the Order which has probably increased with the evolution of politics in the past ten to fifteen years.'

There is also a perception that the standard of candidate entering the Order in more recent years has declined. Phoenix points to a time when prospective members of the Order had to meet certain criteria in terms of religiosity, church attendance and even temperance. 'Today you simply have to declare your loyalist credentials,' he says. 'These people are hoping to use Orangeism for a very different agenda from that which the great and the good historically sought. While Orangeism had a political side, which I feel was overwhelmingly negative, it also had people who joined because of religious values and the whole idea of treating Roman Catholics with respect.' Phoenix believes that those values have been lost specifically by many of the members who joined as a result of the Drumcree crisis.

Some long-standing members of the Order, such as Rev. Brian Kennaway, who was the head of the Grand Lodge Education Committee, have been openly critical of aspects of the institution. Kennaway went so far as to publish a book, *The Orange Order, a Tradition Betrayed*, detailing his concerns over what he sees as a departure from the core values and principles of Orangeism. In it he laments the fact that 'the Institution, once a power within Unionism, came to nothing through a lack of vision and a complete absence of leadership.'

Kennaway also outlines his 'conviction that in many important respects the Order has abandoned basic principles and lost its way, leading to a decline in its membership, influence and public standing. My efforts to achieve reform internally by being pro-active rather than reactive, were thwarted by a cadre of unyielding senior officers.'

He argues rather contentiously that, 'far from being a sectarian, controversial and divisive body, the Order, properly reformed, could be a force for good and reconciliation in Northern Ireland's deeply divided society.'

While many Catholics might have seen that as 'hogwash', many Orangemen saw the book as 'washing the Order's dirty linen in public' and tantamount to betrayal. Other Orangemen took the view that the publication contained important policy analysis and observations and said things that needed to be said.

FACING THE ENEMY

In June 2005, a senior Orangeman from the fiercely loyalist Shankill area of Belfast sat down across a table from a senior republican to discuss parades. District Master Billy Mawhinney was involved in face-to-face exchanges with Seán 'Spike' Murray, who for many years was considered to be one of the most senior figures in the IRA leadership. The talks took place when the unionist North and West Belfast Parades Forum, which included Orangemen, loyalist paramilitaries, politicians and community and church figures met with the nationalist Springfield Road Residents' Action Group.

The 'confidential' meetings involving Billy Mawhinney and Seán Murray were chaired by the Chief Executive of the Community Relations Council, Duncan Morrow. It is understood that they discussed plans for the Whiterock Orange parade in West Belfast, including security, the music to be played, the flags that would be flown and the number of people on parade. The official line was that while 'progress was made, no agreement had been reached'. The crucial aspect, however, was that the meeting had taken place.

Another strand of talking to nationalists involved the Grand Master Robert Saulters and other leading Orangemen who were actively involved in a campaign to preserve and develop the historic Boyne site near Drogheda in County Louth, where the battle was fought between King William and King James. Several field trips took place and, in May 2006, the group ventured even further south to Dublin to meet Martin McAleese, the husband of the President of Ireland. The Orange Order's plan to establish an interpretive centre at the Boyne battleground had attracted his attention. He encouraged the Orangemen to make their case in person in Dublin. When the Grand Lodge officers accepted the invitation, they brought with them several senior Orangemen based in the Republic of Ireland. The delegation met five ministers from the Irish government at the President's residence Áras an Uachtaráin in Phoenix Park.

The discussion broadened out to include concerns over proposals to put a motorway through another important Orange historical site at Aughrim in County Galway. It was here that the bloodiest battle in Ireland involving Williamite and Jacobite forces was fought in 1691, with more than seven thousand combatants killed. The delegation also raised the issue of official recognition of the Orange tradition in the Republic and questioned the refusal of funding applications for seven Orange halls in County Donegal.

Orange Grand Master Robert Saulters is upbeat about the level of contact established that day.

'It was a very good meeting,' he says. 'The southern brethren had complaints about the lack of temporary toilet facilities at Rossnowlagh for their annual Orange parade in County Donegal. There was also the issue of attacks on Orange halls in the Republic.'

The Orangemen were asked which government department they had been dealing with about these matters, but the Orangemen said that they had not contacted any department 'because they felt they wouldn't help them and it was better to keep their heads down'.

'This set the ministers back,' Saulters continues. 'They couldn't get over the fact that these leading Orangemen from the Republic, who they were sitting round the table with, were scared to come near their own government ministers in case it backfired on them. That made an impact. From then on it was a case of "We'll try to help you with this" and "We'll try to help you with that".'

There are about eight hundred Orange halls throughout Ireland and the Orangemen made the case that the buildings were used for other community-based activities and not just lodge meetings. The Orange properties have been targeted for attack on more than 250 occasions from the start of the Troubles, although the vast majority of these attacks happened from the 1980s onwards.

The delegation also requested that consideration be given by the Irish government to establishing a border minorities fund to assist with confidence-building measures among the Protestant minority communities living in the border counties of the Republic. Although Martin McAleese has no official constitutional role, Irish civil servants were present at the meeting, taking notes.

It was not the Orange Grand Master's first visit to Áras an Uachtaráin. In 1999, he and the then Lord Mayor of Belfast, Bob Stoker, had discussed the parades issue with Irish President Mary McAleese. They had also met the Taoiseach (Irish Prime Minister) Bertie Ahern to appraise him of the marching controversy north of the border.

'We met her and the Taoiseach,' Saulters says. 'They thought we [the Orange Order] were backing the Good Friday Agreement, so I told her that we weren't. We also discussed parades such as the one at Ardoyne. There was no animosity and we got on very well. But not all Orangemen north of the border see it that way and I got into trouble for going along to that meeting.'

PARADES LEGISLATION REVIEW

At the end of September 2006, the British government announced a review of the parades legislation in Northern Ireland. While the Orangemen were not exactly throwing their bowler hats into the air in celebration, they were at least quietly satisfied that they had managed to make something happen. Of course the real test would come when the government announced the outcome of the review and what changes, if any, it intended to make. The primary target from the Orange perspective is the Parades Commission – the quasi-judicial decision-making body first set up in 1997 and later legislated under the Public Processions Act (Northern Ireland 1998) – which the Order had grown to loathe over the intervening years.

Before the Commission was established, the police were responsible for making decisions on what restrictions would be placed on parades. It was a task they were only too glad to relinquish. The RUC and later the PSNI still had to police the decisions arrived at by the men and women of the Parades Commission.

The Order views the Commission as anti-Orange. It has regarded the panel of seven government appointees as a group of people whose job is to stop Loyal Order parades and put obstacles in the way of anyone trying to celebrate Protestant culture.

A talks process about the parades problem was set in motion and lasted eighteen months. It involved the Loyal Orders and government officials. The Orders criticised the lack of transparency over the Parades Commission rulings, pointing out that when restrictions were placed on a parade, the explanation given usually included the line 'because of public order concerns'. It was argued that this played directly into the hands of those bent on causing trouble, as opposed to genuine residents. Some unionist politicians have described it as a 'rioters' charter'.

In 2006, the Orange Order, the Black Institution and the Independent Orange Order comprised the Joint Loyal Orders Working Group, which was involved in a series of ground breaking meetings with nationalist politicians north and south of the border. The JLOWG said that the discussions were part of an ongoing dialogue to explain why the Orders believe that the Parades Commission should be replaced.

In June, the Working Group met the most senior Catholic clergyman in Ireland, Archbishop Seán Brady. The Loyal Orders delegation consisted of Robert Saulters and Drew Nelson from the Grand Lodge of Ireland, William Logan and the Rev. Tom Greer of the Royal Black Institution, and George Dawson MLA and Mervyn Storey MLA from the Independent Orange Institution.

Following the meeting, the group issued a press statement which read:

> The Joint Loyal Orders Working Group met today with Archbishop Sean Brady and other representatives of the Roman Catholic church as part of its ongoing dialogue to explain why it believes the Parades Commission should be replaced by a more equitable system for regulating public events.

A spokesman for the Joint Working Group described the meeting as 'cordial, businesslike and a useful exchange of views, held in an atmosphere of concern for the coming months which all sides wish to see pass in an entirely peaceful manner.'

What was astonishing was not that the meeting had been 'cordial' but that it had taken place at all. These were Orangemen whose base qualifications state that they should 'strenuously oppose the fatal errors and doctrines of the Church of Rome and scrupulously avoid countenancing (by their presence or otherwise) any act or ceremony of Popish worship … and by all lawful means, resist the ascendancy of that Church

… and the extension of its power.' It was remarkable because this was a very public 'official meeting' with the Catholic Primate, but it was not the first time that senior Orangemen had met the Archbishop. The Orange Order had been in touch with the Catholic Church leader during some of the worst years of the Drumcree protests.

The Working Group also met representatives of the Irish Department of Foreign Affairs and the SDLP along with unionist politicians, the Secretary of State and the Human Rights Commission. The Loyal Orders were making it clear to anyone who would listen that they wanted the Parades Commission scrapped and replaced by what they would regard as a more equitable regulating body.

The former Church of Ireland Primate Lord Eames believes that any review looking at parading in the future needs to be as broad as possible.

'I think there has to be a new overall strategy on culture as well as on parades,' he says. 'Parading is part of the Protestant culture, but we shouldn't allow protests to become part of that culture too. If you can get a meeting point for the two traditions in Northern Ireland you could have peaceful parades, peaceful acknowledgement that the parade was part of the other side's culture and if it's not going to threaten you, then your protest diminishes.'

Later in 2006, the Secretary of State for Northern Ireland, Peter Hain, wrote to the leadership of the Loyal Orders – the Orange, the Black and the Apprentice Boys – announcing what he called a 'fairly wide-ranging consideration which could include legislation, if there was consensus in favour of that'.

Northern Ireland Office Minister Paul Goggins was appointed to take the project forward and the invitations went out for a range of views on what the terms of reference of the review should be. The project was described as a 'longer-term, strategic look at parading'. The review was given a qualified welcome by the Orders and the main unionist parties. The DUP described it as a first step. Ian Paisley was quoted in the *Belfast Newsletter* as saying, 'There can be no role for the Parades Commission and any terms of reference of this review must be sufficiently wide to allow for a new way of dealing with parading.'

The same newspaper quoted outspoken Orangeman David McNarry of the Ulster Unionist Party who said, 'We need to scrap the Commission and replace it with a group of people who understand and respect the historical position that Loyal Order parades play in the life of Northern Ireland.'

It has been suggested by some media commentators that if the Parades Commission is replaced, the man to lead whatever succeeds it is Lord Eames, although his involvement with the unsuccessful attempts to resolve the Drumcree dispute means that he will be perceived by some to have 'baggage'. Lord Eames has his own views on how the parades issue should be handled.

I am not certain if the present structure of the Parades Commission will succeed,' he says. 'I think there may well be an avenue for something else that would allow the Orange Order to engage in dialogue and feel that their voices are being heard ... I've never said I want the

Commission replaced, but I want to get as much realism on the ground for dealing with parades. I know the issue was discussed during the St Andrews talks but I have not had it [heading up an alternative body] mentioned to me by anyone and I would have to think very long and hard about it. I want to do what I can for all the people of Northern Ireland and if that role was an opportunity, I would take it seriously. But I need to be certain that it wouldn't be another Bertha McDougal situation whereby you are shot into something and there were political ramifications from it.

Neil Jarman of the Institute for Conflict Research believes that some people are beginning to 'wise-up' in the midst of all the controversy surrounding parades.

I think people have realised that parades are a sore point on both sides and that they have the potential in certain circumstances to take Northern Ireland to the edge, as they did in 1996–97. We weren't too far away then from an outright eruption of much more sustained violence at that time.

Jarman hopes that people have moved back from that position.

'I don't think there is any way that the parades dispute could be re-ignited to the extent it was then because the political context is not the same,' he says.

THE THAW SETS IN

Senior Orangemen were now meeting senior republicans, and other members of the Order were also involved in unofficial and discreet contacts with representatives of Sinn Féin. A thaw appeared to be settling on some parts of the institution. The return of devolved government to Stormont would mean Sinn Féin having a major say in the running of Northern Ireland. This posed the very real possibility of the Orange Order, if it wanted to do business at the highest level with the people that mattered, finding itself in official face-to-face meetings with Sinn Féin government ministers.

'Who knows what sort of government we are going to have here?' says Robert Saulters. 'After meeting with the SDLP I was asked would I never speak to Sinn Féin and I said, "I never say never." That didn't go down too well.'

Neil Jarman says that the Grand Lodge policy of refusing to meet Sinn Féin does not always converge with the actions of individual Orangemen and private lodges. He cites Newtown-butler as one of the rare examples of Orangemen getting involved in such discussions and reaching a compromise. However, there have been other examples.

'In quieter, smaller parades, I think it's the local lodges saying, "This is our village, this is our town, and we are not going to be dictated to by somewhere else",' he explains. 'In the same way as a lot of Orangemen walked away from the Drum-cree protest because they saw it as Portadown's fight, not theirs … they didn't want to ruin existing community relations in their own towns and villages.'

In mid-April 2007 the Secretary of State, Peter Hain,

announced that the former Liberal Democrat leader Lord Ashdown would chair the long-awaited independent review of parading issues in Northern Ireland. The Strategic Review of Parades Body also included leading west Belfast republican Sean 'Spike' Murray. The DUP described Murray's appointment as potentially disastrous. Sinn Féin expressed reservations about Paddy Ashdown's role, given that he had once served in Northern Ireland as an officer in the British army. The most telling response however came from the Orange Order. A statement from the Grand Lodge of Ireland simply welcomed the announcement of the review body, which it sees as another step towards the eventual scrapping of the Parades Commission. The review body is not due to report back until some time in 2008 so deciding on contentious parades for the 2007 marching season still rests with the Parades Commission. However the writing is on the wall for the Commission. Its days are numbered and despite the initial predictable political protestations, it's likely the Strategic Review will be given a fair wind by those keen to see either a resolution of the parades issue, the demise of the Parades Commission or both.

AN ORDER IN DECLINE?

The institution is cagey about its membership figures. When asked a direct question as to how many Orangemen there are in Ireland, senior officers usually keep that card close to their collarettes. Notionally the Order at one time would have claimed a hundred thousand members, but the figure is now believed to be below fifty thousand and some would put it as low as thirty thousand.

'It no longer has that cross-class element,' says Eamon Phoenix. He continues:

> As an historian looking on, I think Orangeism is in terminal decline and there are only certain ways it can go. One is to repackage itself and build bridges to the entire community and I think there are elements within the institution trying to do that. There are Orangemen who want to visit schools of all denominations to explain the origins of the Order and acknowledge that it has a certain commonality with other brotherhoods in Ireland, such as the Ancient Order of Hibernians. Nobody contests the fact that Orangeism has played a very important role in the history of Ireland, and an element in the membership is seeking to shift the spotlight off the contentious parade routes and onto the cultural heritage trail.

'These Orangemen are seeking to move in a much more modern direction in terms of valuing their culture while cleaning up their act,' explains Phoenix. 'Similarly there are those members who see the Order as serving a sort of Drumcree agenda and inevitably as they pursue that, others within Orangeism will raise their voices against it.'

The Grand Master, Robert Saulters, has been the target of much criticism from people outside and inside the institution. He has been painted as a fence-sitter, slow to react and weak at times when the Order needed strong leadership. At the end of 2006, he was re-elected to continue as the head of the Orange Order, and he may soon find himself facing the dilemma of having to decide whether or not to engage in face-to-face talks with Sinn Féin. A power-sharing executive at Stormont including the DUP and Sinn Féin will change the political landscape historically and irrevocably.

At the Grand Lodge of Ireland meeting in Belfast in March 2006, the brethren reaffirmed their policy of not meeting with the Parades Commission and not meeting with Sinn Féin-controlled residents' groups. Six months later, however, a level of pragmatism had entered into the Grand Master's thinking when he conceded during an interview with the author that he might have to meet with the political party Orangemen blame for trying to destroy Orange culture.

'Of course I may have to speak to Sinn Féin ministers at Stormont,' says the Grand Master. Surprisingly he appears to hold a more prognostic view, believing that a power-sharing environment would make such an event much more likely.

'Of course it would,' he says. 'If the government of the country was up and running and they're all sitting together up at Stormont … Gerry Kelly could even be the Security Minister. But that's up to the people we've voted into politics. It could happen. You never know what's going to happen in this country.'

Some Orangemen argue that a meeting of this kind between the Order and Sinn Féin will never happen and that if it does, it will be 'over my dead body'. Many fear that it could be the final nail in the coffin for Orangeism. The same voices probably said something similar a few years ago about meetings with the Irish government and the leader of the Catholic Church. Historically there have always been grumbling voices and dissent within the ranks of the Orange Order, but somehow the institution has survived when other organisations would have folded.

Neil Jarman believes that longevity is one of the Orange Order's strengths.

'You could say it's probably outlived all other institutions in the Protestant community in Ireland,' he explains. 'There's a continuity there that no other organisation has provided over that period of time and it looks like it's going to outlive the Ulster Unionist party as well.'

He believes that as long as the Order retains its current degree of popular support, it can probably continue.

'You can't deny the historical importance of the organisation,' he says. 'It provides a sense of community, and it's one of those organisations that gives a degree of surety about what you are. It indicates what it is to be a Protestant in Northern Ireland even though a lot of people have very different ideas about what that is.'

Lord Trimble believes that the Orange Order is in no danger of disappearing from the Northern Ireland landscape.

'It's too big and too broad in terms of its influence within society here,' according to the former UUP leader. 'Change has to happen and the Order has to come more into the modern world and it also needs to acknowledge that Vatican II has happened. That's something which a lot of Orangemen and a lot of Protestants in Northern Ireland haven't actually factored into their minds, the extent to which Catholicism has changed. That change took place quite some time ago and it's a significant factor that needs to be borne in mind.'

It is the diverse nature of the Orange Order's membership,

its long and turbulent history, its ability to heal itself just when it appears mortally wounded and its capacity at times to do the unthinkable that makes meeting these challenges and even doing business with Sinn Féin in the not-too-distant future, a distinct possibility.

If the institution is sincere about modernising and accentuating its culture, history and heritage over the less palatable aspects, hard work, a greater openness, sincerity and time will be required to convince a naturally sceptical and increasingly pluralist society. The days of playing the Orange Card are over. Equal Opportunity legislation outlaws favouritism or unfair influence in the workplace. Most importantly, with Irish republicanism, in the shape of Sinn Féin, now the second largest body politic north of the border, Northern Ireland is on the cusp of change, the like of which has not been seen since partition.

That will necessitate alterations in the establishment and it will also require a shift in mindset by those seriously intent on engaging with the new political system and the re-alignment of society in Northern Ireland that will be a consequence of it. The Orange Institution, like the other Loyal Orders, has to ask itself whether or not it has a future in a new Northern Ireland and, if it does, what that future will be.

Brian Kennaway's book – *The Orange Order, A Tradition Betrayed* – cites the ritual expression of traditional values for Orangemen:

> We must all endeavour to disarm suspicion and antagonism. This can best be done by setting a good example in our daily lives, by living up to the high priniciples of the

Order so that every section of the community will be compelled to admit that there is something in the Orange Society that elevates a man and raises him above the average of humanity. Something that makes him a better man morally, socially and intellectually.

Behind the collarettes and under the bowler hats there are many good and honourable men yet within the ranks of Orangeism there are also dishonourable members. Despite the laudable community service work, the large sums of money raised for charity and no matter how convincingly the Orange culture card is played, the good men will still find themselves being dragged into the dock by the misdeeds of their less virtuous brethren. The days of 'Not an inch' and 'Not an ounce', 'No surrender' and '*Tiocfaidh Ár Lá*' are fast receding amidst a welter of political, economic and even European regeneration. Orangeism is struggling to find its place and its voice in this new scenario and, if the culture is to locate a continuum for the rest of the twenty-first century and beyond, it will require strength in leadership, humility in adversity, generosity of spirit and the courage of its Protestant convictions.

A large swathe of public opinion on both sides of the border would judge that some of these qualities were displayed very publicly on Monday 26 March 2007. In one amazing moment in the political history of Ireland and Great Britain, the Democratic Unionist Party leader Ian Paisley sat down beside Sinn Féin President Gerry Adams and jointly announced a power sharing administration at Stormont would be up and running by 8 May, just six weeks later. The jaw dropping sight of Paisley and Adams in close proximity and singing off the same political hymn sheet left many people stunned and astonished. Even among those who saw it there were some who could not believe it. For a number of local councillors and the party's MEP, it was too much to stomach and the move prompted their resignations from the DUP.

Dissident republicans saw Adams' gesture as a sell-out. After thirty years of 'armed struggle' to get the British out of Ireland here was the figurehead of the republican movement doing a deal with the man who embodied unflinching unionism and Britishness throughout the period of the conflict. The two political leaders talked of a new era in Northern Ireland politics, of a true and lasting peace and Gerry Adams referred to a new relationship between 'the Orange and the Green.' The fact that these two men were able to do what they did means that anything is possible. If the power sharing arrangements are successful and all the parties live up to the electorate's democratic expectations, this will change the political and socio-economic climate of Northern Ireland probably forever.

No one who supports the process wants the residual acrimony that is represented by Drumcree, Ardoyne, or any other flashpoint area, to destabilise the situation. It is not unreasonable to expect a degree of lateral thinking on these and other contentious issues. After a period of history punctuated by discord, hatred and violence, it may be a startlingly optimistic note on which to conclude, yet opportunities may arise to put the culture of Orangeism on a more positive footing. The new political dispensation holds the potential to secure Orange traditions for future generations making the institution a living breathing body rather than a dusty old corpse. For many brethren a successful outcome would be a victory for pragmatism without necessarily surrendering on principle. The challenge will be for those within the loyal Order to recognise the opportunities when they present themselves, to seize them and exploit them to the betterment of Orangeism, but not to the detriment of everyone else in Northern Ireland.

After generations of two traditions marching in opposite directions or into conflict with each other, the 'war in Ireland' is coming to an end and a peaceful co-existence appears to be just beginning. The IRA is melting into the background and the loyalist paramilitaries are slowly following it. New ways of 'walking and talking' are just starting to emerge. Tomorrow, next week, next month and next year may well see people from both the Orange and Green communities taking bold steps in a joint parade – a parade into the unknown.

PEOPLE, POLITICS AND POWER

Stephen Collins

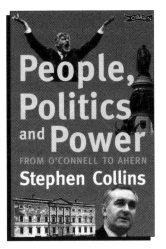

Politics in Ireland is something of a national obsession. Despite a decline in voter turnout in recent general elections, politics still attracts huge interest and controversy. Powerful political figures like Charles Haughey, Eamon de Valera, Charles Stewart Parnell and Daniel O'Connell dominated Irish politics at different times over the past two centuries and defined their eras. The great election campaigns waged by these politicians, and the controversies in which they were involved, have left a deep imprint on all aspects of Irish life, from law to literature; from economics to family life.

This book gives us a concise overview of Irish political life, from the Act of Union to the present day.

THE STOLEN VILLAGE

Des Ekin

In June 1631 pirates from Algiers and armed troops of the Turkish Ottoman Empire, led by the notorious pirate captain Morat Rais, stormed ashore at the little harbour village of Baltimore in West Cork. They captured almost all the villagers and bore them away to a life of slavery in North Africa. The prisoners were destined for a variety of fates — some would live out their days chained to the oars as galley slaves, while others would spend long years in the scented seclusion of the harem or within the walls of the Sultan's palace.

The old city of Algiers, with its narrow streets, intense heat and lively trade, was a melting pot where the villagers would join slaves and freemen of many nationalities. Only two of them ever saw Ireland again.

The Stolen Village is a fascinating tale of international piracy and culture clash nearly 400 years ago and is the first book to cover this relatively unknown and under-researched incident in Irish history.

O'BRIEN POCKET HISTORY OF IRELAND

Breandán O hEithir

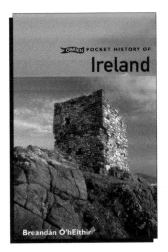

New edition of this short and entertaining history from earliest times to the present by one of Ireland's best-loved writers. It deals with prehistory, the Celts, Christianity, the Vikings, the Normans. The various conquests and rebellions are covered, including Cromwell, Wolfe Tone, the 1916 Rising. One of the main features is that it brings history up to date, providing an interesting account of both North and South over the past eighty years, clarifying the development and intricacies of the Northern 'troubles' and the many attempts to resolve them. Understanding and sympathetic, this little book gives a clear and stimulating grasp of Ireland, past and present.

O'BRIEN POCKET HISTORY OF IRISH WRITERS

A. Norman Jeffares

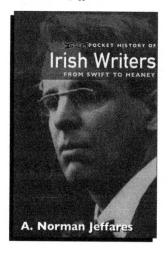

This book includes all the leading Irish writers and some of the lesser known: playwrights, novelists, short story writers, poets. It places them in context and provides a list of their works. Commentaries give brief but telling insights into their work.

The story of Irish writing is followed, beginning with Swift, and working through playwrights Synge and O'Casey to Beckett and Friel; in novels, from Maria Edgeworth, through Joyce, Elizabeth Bowen, Kate O'Brien, Flann O'Brien to contemporaries Julia O'Faolain and Roddy Doyle; from nineteenth-century poetry through Yeats to Paul Durcan.

O'BRIEN POCKET HISTORY OF IRISH SAINTS

Brian Lacey

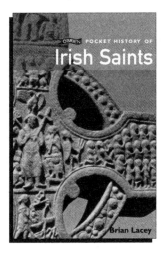

Early Irish records list as many as 1,700 saints. There is a wealth of folklore, legend and tradition and literature associated with them. These colourful characters taught, looked after the sick, settled feuds, wrote histories and poetry. Some endured incredible hardship, living in hermitages on barren cliff tops, such as on Skellig. Many, such as Cillian and Columbanus, travelled thousands of miles to spread the Christian faith, establishing large, powerful monasteries across Europe.

This book provides a fascinating anthology of the lives and times of Ireland's holy men and women. Accessible in style, with plenty of anecdotal evidence, it gives an insight into the early origins of Christianity and the role of the religious in Irish society.

ENDURANCE

Dermot Somers

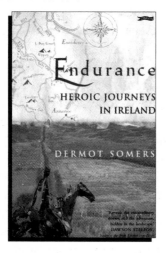

Kidnap, jailbreak, power, faith, murder, betrayal, scholarship, survival and above all, sheer endurance — all are themes in Dermot Somers' stories of heroic and historic travels from the mythic legends of prehistory to the dawn of modern Ireland. With the aid of maps and photographs, Dermot Somers — mountaineer, Gaelic scholar, TV presenter, and writer — follows in the footsteps of these epic journeys, revealing the people, the cultures, the times, the places and the echoes surviving in our landscape — from Art O'Neill's icy grave in the Wicklow mountains to the ringfort-hiding place of the brown bull in the secret valley of the Cooley Mountains.

EXPLORING NEWGRANGE

Liam Mac Uistin

Older than the Egyptian pyramids, older than Stonehenge, for 5,000 years the ancient megalithic tomb at Newgrange in County Meath has housed the remains of Stone Age 'aristocracy', sheltering the spirits of the long dead from the outside world. This book explores the creation, building and discovery of Newgrange. Why did these people spend years building this tomb? How did they move huge boulders miles across hilly country and erect them at the site, without the aid of machinery? Modern archaeological techniques have revealed much about the lives of our Stone Age ancestors, but Newgrange still retains many of its secrets. *Exploring Newgrange* uncovers, in words and illustrations, the extent, and limitations, of our knowledge of this world-famous site.